Go Away to the Edge of Borneo

Rachant Srisakulchawla

Red | Motorcycle
PUBLISHING HOUSE

A path that is not directed by others, but that which is blazed by themselves.

A path that's not intended to be understood, or followed -- but one that is absolutely for self-contentment.

After getting the motorcycle back, I immediately took it to show it off to my grandma.

"Isn't it beautiful? It's bright red."

With love and affection, but perhaps with slightly spiked blood-pressure, she said,

"Oh! My word! I told you to change it to a red car."

Go Away to the Edge of Borneo

Contents

Introduction

Chapter 1 Riding a Motorcycle Far Away to Please a Woman

This story is purely fiction. It did not happen. Should there be any resemblance to actual persons or events, please understand that it is a coincidence ... without a doubt a mere coincidence.

Everyone knows that 'Nusara' is everything to me. Nusara herself also knows, but sometimes she is still not satisfied. To quote Gu Long (Go Leng in Thai), the maestro of contemporary Chinese martial arts novels,

'A woman who has been pleased by a man since bygone days knows no bounds to her own satisfaction.'

On some instances she could no longer stand me and told me to go away. And that's it, to please her, I had to ride off on my motorcycle far, far, away.

I had a lot of fun and Nusara was pleased to distance herself from her man for a while. The man satisfied, the woman happy – What can be a more perfect world?

Nusara is really my everything. If I want to drink coffee, she would make me a perfect espresso shot. She learned her barista skills from (Café) Amazon and was even the champion of her class.

Whether I have a craving for 'baked spaghetti with cheese' or 'omelet rice without eggs' (she really can cook this), she would whip up these dishes. And sometimes when we are enjoying ourselves watching TV, I would ask her to fetch me a glass of water and hold it for me because my hands aren't free as I haven't yet finished eating. She is ready to be my cup holder.

1

Whenever I feel too lazy to attend a meeting, she would go in my stead. When I feel an itch in my back, she would scratch it for me. When I'm stressed from work, she would be my sounding board and talk to me. When she goes shopping, I go off to ride my motorcycle. When she is stressed, I go off for a ride on my motorcycle. When she wants to go somewhere, she would drive herself because I would be gone with my motorcycle. We have such a perfect married life.

Until one day I was curious and asked her, "Nusara, when I'm away for many days, are you happy?"

"Yes," she answered.

"And when I'm around, are you happy too?"

"Yes," she answered.

"And which way are you happier?"

Nusara was silent for over half a day before she finally responded, "You don't want to know."

Everyone knows that I like to please her ... and to keep her happy, so, I don't want to know.

Sometimes when she was overwhelmed by too much of "my everything", she would "radiate a certain evil aura". And if she was still to be more of "my everything", she would start ranting and raving and ending the sentence with,

"Go away!"

To please her ... I have to go away...far.

Riding my motorcycle off far and away.

From the City of Chiang Mai to Samoeng, Lampang, Wiang Pa Pao, Phrao, Mae Khachan, Wang Nuea, Phayao... Still, this is not far enough for Nusara.

'A woman who has been pleased by a man since bygone days knows no bounds to her own satisfaction.'

Once in a while, Nusara would still say, "Go away."

If she said "go the same distance as last time," I would understand that, Okay, this distance was already far enough, but she didn't say that.

As far as Sukhothai, Phitsanulok, she still said "Go away."

Kanchanaburi or Siem Reap, "Go away."

Hoi An, Nha Jang, Mui Ne, "Go away."

Penang, Terengganu, "Go away."

Johor Bahru, "Go away."

Go all the way right to the furthest tip of Singapore until one can see all the way to Indonesia in the distance, Nusara would still say, "Go away."

I thought it was already quite far. This was already quite a lot of letting her have her way.

'A woman who has been pleased by a man since bygone days knows no bounds to her own satisfaction.'

But then, everyone knows that Rachant thrives on pleasing and doting on Nusara. So, if she still thinks that Singapore is not far enough, I have prepared the route to East Malaysia, Brunei and Indonesia, especially to please her.

I only recently learned that Malaysia is divided into East Malaysia and West Malaysia, separated by a large sea. The Malaysia we are familiar with, is on the west side, where the capital city of Kuala Lumpur and cities that are familiar among Thais such as Penang, Malacca and Johor Bahru are located. East Malaysia comprises the state of Sabah which has Kota Kinabalu as a famous tourist destination, the state of Sarawak, and the Labuan Federation.

Borneo is home to East Malaysia, and on this same island is also the location of the country of Brunei and parts of Indonesia. The island is very famous for its abundance of nature, wildlife, orangutans and beautiful seas.

I tried to go to this island myself on a motorcycle trip before, but couldn't find a ferry to cross over. When I stumbled upon an offer for a 10-day motorcycle tour, along this same route, I made inquiries and asked for the details about the ferry crossing. I found the tour program quite interesting, good accommodation, not too great a distance to ride each day, and it also covers three countries. Before making reservations, I asked three additional difficult questions

"Can I not ride off-road?"

"Yes."

"Can I not ride too fast?"

"Yes."

"I am a vegetarian. Can you accommodate me? "

"Yes."

Everything was perfect! So, I paid the money in order to go far away... To please Nusara.

But the tour had fixed dates and times. Should Nusara happen to throw a tantrum telling me to "Go away," without looking at the date it would really be a hassle. So, I schemed to make Nusara increasingly "my everything" ... "my utmost" everything at any opportune time. I let her take care of the children, the house, the company finances, the construction of two hotels, and prepared for her to take care of the home improvement project.

I couldn't help thinking to myself that I was so unfortunate having to keep on pleasing Nusara to make her "my everything" to such an extreme. There were so many complications. The more I thought about them, the dizzier I got...Slowly, I started to pack my bag, and send my trusted buddy, the yellow Ducati motorcycle on a pick-up truck over to Had Yai.

When Nusara said, "Go away," on February 21st, the next morning of February 22nd, I immediately had to oblige Nusara's wishes.

Embarking on the journey right away.

Part 1: Logistics Ride

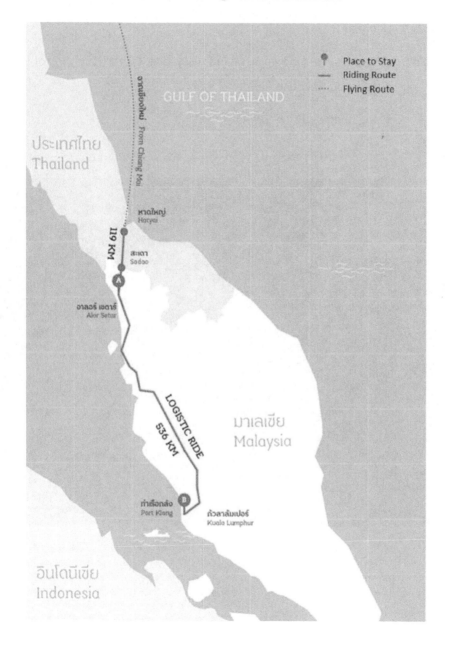

Chapter 2 Riding a Motorcycle, Ripping Your Heart in Two

The tour company that organized my trip to Borneo had excellent profiting schemes. I came to learn about their dazzling tricks from the first day until the last day of my journey. Had I known beforehand, I wouldn't have got mixed up with them.

Their scheme was very simple -- by writing 2 items in fine print at the bottom of the application.

Number one, the company reserves the right to change the schedule and all the programs at their discretion.

Number two, no refunds will be given under any circumstances.

With these rules set, the company would change the schedule back and forth as deemed appropriate (or so they claimed), but the truth was to lure people so that they couldn't make it in time and had to cancel. Then, the company would refuse to give them a refund, and make all the profit.

The first trick was the change of the ferry schedule to Borneo. On February 16th the tour operator confirmed that we had to take our motorcycle over to Port Klang on February 28th before 5 p.m. So, my plan was to send the Ducati over in a truck on the 21st and hoped to pick it up on the 28th but the plans got changed quite unexpectedly. It turned out that the bike had to arrive at Port Klang on February 24th at 5 p.m. instead.

The plane ticket also had to be changed. The motorcycle transfer schedule had to be changed. My first plan to ride around to tour Malaysia for a couple of days before sending my motorcycle to Port Klang had to be canceled. As it turned out, I had to ride all the way from Hat Yai to Port Klang in twenty-six hours. The sightseeing mission was changed to a logistical ride.

The plane landed at 3 p.m. The scheduled pick-up for the car and the Ducati in Hat Yai was about the same time. It turned out that the truck had broken down the night before and had to be switched and it was expected to arrive three hours late. So, all in all, there were only 23 hours left to get the motorcycle across the border to Port Klang.

The driving distance from Hat Yai city to Port Klang was about 561 kilometers. If everything went according to plan, I would have done it in one day. But if we encountered problems like rainstorms, flat tires, running out of gas or whatever, the money I paid for the tour, the motorcycle transfer, and the trip to Borneo would just be gone in the blink of an eye.

Go Away to the Edge of Borneo

Today, I set a goal to reach Alor Setar, the hometown of Mr. Mahathir[1], the senior prime minister of Malaysia. It isn't too far but can take off about 100 kilometers of the entire distance and is already considered to be across the border.

The intention to ride the motorcycle in low risk like what I've always done was a no-go for this trip because I had to ride at night, cross the border at night, and I needed to speed up. I had to leave Hat Yai at about 6 p.m., and stop to pick up customs documents along the way. By the time I reached Sadao checkpoint, the sky was already pitch black.

After reaching the checkpoint on the Thai side, I parked the car in front of the building where I would get my passport stamped and went to use the restroom. While in the restroom, I heard the sound of people talking, mentioning a "Thai motorcycle". I hurried out to look. I knew it ... The bag was opened. Someone had snuck over to open my luggage, I hurriedly moved the car, got my passport stamped, and checked my bags. I wasn't too afraid of missing things but afraid of getting something extra. When I didn't find anything, I decided to journey on.

Across the Malaysian border at Bukit Kayu Hitam checkpoint, I was warmly welcomed as usual. In less than ten minutes, the yellow Ducati was already roaring menacingly on the E1 Expressway -- a 500-kilometer-long highway that starts in the South of Thailand, which also happens to be the northernmost region of Malaysia, and ends in the central region of Malaysia, where the capital city of Kuala Lumpur is located.

On the expressway, there are no traffic lights, no U-turns, no potholes. It's a great road for which motorcycle aficionados yearn. Not only that, while cars are required to pay toll fees, for motorcycles, it's a free ride the whole way.

The tension I had encountered at the checkpoint started to melt away on the E1 and after a few detours around Alor Setar, the yellow Ducati and its master finally reached the city.

I stopped to admire the city's famous black mosque, the Zahir Mosque, whose black dome shimmers in the night lights -- the beauty and faith of the people in Muslim countries. Not far away was Alor Setar Tower, a tall, prominent, brightly lit tower with the same name as the city, exuding cheery and vibrant vibes.

It was 10:30 p.m. Malaysia time (an hour ahead to that of Thailand), the Ducati and its master had just checked in to a hotel near the city's beautiful tower. Today's total distance covered was 118.8 kilometers.

The next day I woke up early and started the journey right away. Breakfast could wait. I had to ride for about 460 kilometers to arrive at my destination before 5 p.m. So, I headed on to Malaysia's beautifully paved E1 Expressway without delay.

The pleasure of riding at dawn is to experience the soft sunlight and the peacefulness of people's slow-pace. I spent time on my motorcycle happily riding along, until the Ducati cried hungry through all of her dials on the dashboard, so her master turned into a gas station to feed her a full tank of exquisite, 100-octane wine - - the best wine it ever tasted.

Shortly after leaving the gas station, we passed the bustling city of Penang. I slowed down because of heavy traffic on the highway. After Penang, the road became a long straight stretch again. The Ducati roared melodiously. Her master kept on delivering commands through his right hand for the air-cooled two-cylinder engine to continuously churn out galloping horses. After a long straight road, we worked our way up the mountain to Ipoh. The 1,079-cc yellow Ducati, with its signature spring-free valve system, pushed forward, leaning into the spectacular curves on the smooth pavement, surrounded by tall mountains, and countless palm trees. There was some light fog. The weather was pleasant. It was a perfect morning, exceptional dash, excellent valves, magnificent Italian horse. We then reached a marvelous tunnel.

The tunnel ... was a full orchestra, a dream rock concert, a screeching guitar solo tune ripping apart the hearts of aficionados of melodious motorcycles around the world.

The eight-hundred-meters long tunnel was called the Minora Tunnel. Two years ago, in March, I rode the melodious two-cylinder, "flower that loves to caress the wind", red Triumph over the entire trip of more than 5,200 kilometers and dashed through this 800-meter long tunnel. This was where the sound was the sweetest.

This time, it was the two-cylinder, gangster-sounding yellow Ducati's turn.

I slowed down, maintaining a safe distance from the car ahead. And as soon as I got out of the sun and into the rocky mountains, my left hand squeezed the clutch, my left foot slapped down two gears. Then, I released the clutch, while activating the accelerator with the right hand sending the 100-octane wine through the injection and cool air into the cave of antique valves. The engine produced horse powers and relayed them to the knobby wheels while blasting sound through the original, factory-made twin exhaust pipes. Even without the upgrade, the ear-piercing sound was blaring and cutting deep into the heart -- hurting so good.

The sound of the two-cylinder engine in my memory stirred a melodiously mournful mood reminiscent of the Guns N 'Roses concert. If it were a song, it would be a ballad like November Rain or Don't Cry while this bad-ass, two-cylinder belted a reverberating, wild roar like You Could Be Mine. Yesssssss ... Arghhhhhhhhh ... and I'll rip your heart in two.

Chapter 3 The Toilet that Made a Thai Man Think Twice

Descending from the mountain through Ipoh, my next destination was Kuala Lumpur.

I thought there was still time, so I took an exit from the expressway to ride on a small local road, B4^2, passing a beautiful billboard with the words SIME DARBY PLANTATION on it. Last time I was here, I also saw a lot of signs like this, both on and off the highway. Curiosity made me look it up and found that this is actually the largest oil palm company in the world. With more than 6.25 million rai (.2.47 million acres -- A rai is a Thai unit of area that equals to 1,600 square meters or 0.3954 acres, and is used in measuring land area) of plantation land in 17 countries (including Thailand), their CPO (crude palm oil) capacity accounts for 4% of the global CPO production capacity. No wonder why the billboards are so stylish and can be seen everywhere in Malaysia.

On the way, I stopped to eat vegetarian food in Selangor. It was truly delicious. Once my stomach was full and my hunger satiated, I headed straight to a coffee shop called Klang Espresso, named after the city Klang. The distance from there to my next destination was less than 30 kilometers and it wouldn't take more than 45 minutes as estimated by Google Maps. It was a little after 1 p.m. which meant I'd have enough time to drink my coffee leisurely for about fifteen minutes.

When I parked in front of the coffee shop, the door was locked. The glass was darkly tinted and I couldn't see anything inside. After a few minutes, someone came to the door and let me in. Was this a coffee shop, a casino or some secret hideaway? Once inside, I saw a lot of people there including children and teenagers. A young barista was busy at work at the counter.

She had an interesting personality -- Highly enthusiastic and very cute-looking. She had the appearance like that of a typical Malaysian girl of Chinese descent. Her coffee menu was too complicated to be understood by a lay person who's not a coffee connoisseur like me, so I asked the pretty barista for a recommendation.

"I'd like a hot Americano. Could you recommend something?"

"This coffee is planted in Klang, the beans are also roasted in Klang," A very good suggestion.

Coffee grown in Klang, roasted in Klang, brewed in Klang, served in Klang by a pretty barista from Klang. Without asking any further, I knew immediately she was from Klang because of the pride that resonated in her voice.

After placing my order, I went to the restroom. Once I had opened the door, I was stunned... and for one moment could hardly move. I simply couldn't imagine in what position I was going to relieve myself. After all these years in my life I had never encountered a toilet this complicated. Finally, I decided to use the women's bathroom with a Thai man's standard pose.

Then, I came out to drink my coffee. It was marvelously brewed, its taste so refined. All the while I was drinking my coffee, there was always someone knocking on the glass, knocking on the door. The cute barista was the only staff working at the time. Sometimes she opened the door in time and sometimes she didn't. Sometimes the customers helped open it. I kept observing things and was wondering why a coffee shop had to be so secretive -- the doors, the bathroom, and the coffee beans.So, I had a chat with the lovely barista.

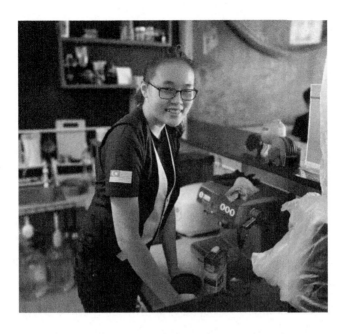

Her name was Joey, a native of Klang, born and raised. She truly loved her hometown and wished many people came to visit. Another thing she loved was coffee. She aspired to be a professional barista. Joey's dream was of becoming partners with the owner, or maybe opening her own place with her sister in the future.

"The front door is a matter of safety. Because I'm alone. This way, I can see who's coming, and if I'm comfortable enough to let them in", Joey explained. I didn't get to talk about the bathroom before she had to go back to her barista duties behind the counter.

She had determination, clarity, love and passion about what she was doing. This kind of person would go on to fulfill her dream of being a coffee shop owner in the future and she could be anything and much more on the path that she had chosen.

At about two o'clock, the Americano was now in my system   and it was time to continue my journey.

The tour company was still vehemently on track with their strategy 'to block people from arriving on time" by indicating GPS coordinates that are different from the name of the place.

I followed the map to the pinned destination by place name, so I ended up in the wrong place! By the time I realized that the right location was another 30 kilometers away, there was less than two hours left to take the motorcycle to the ferry at Port Klang in time.

Complaining was useless. I realized I had better start traveling.

The road was under construction. Hundreds of thousands of big rigs towing containers in the back parked in a long line. The weather was hot and humid. The yellow Ducati transformed into a barbecue grill with its master's calves laid over it. The heat spread from those calves to my heart...It was burning.

The beefy hips of the Gangster Yellow and a large suitcase made matter worse. I had to try so hard to duck and zigzag through a narrow gap. It was nice to get cooperation from the big-wheelers. When I signaled for them to give me some space, they happily moved. Around 4:20 p.m., the yellow Ducati brought its bruised and battered master to his destination.

The logistics riding mission was completed with 536.4 kilometers -- beating the tour company's profiting scheme by arriving just 40 minutes before the appointment.

The yellow Ducati still had a mission to continue on by boarding a ferry bound for Borneo. Its master headed for Kuala Lumpur Airport to fly directly to Chiang Mai. Before parting, we said goodbye. "See you in ten days, you barbecue grill, yellow Ducati."

Though you're hot, I still love you.

While sitting on the plane, I thought about Joey's coffee shop -- the coffee might have been   excellent but I didn't think of the coffee. The barista might have been cute and charming but it wasn't her I was thinking of. My only thought was about the bathroom.

Lean left. Lean right. Stand. Turn around. Slowly stand up. Crouch down. Crouch down while leaning left...Ouch! Why must it be so complicated, Joey?

Part 2: Tour Ride

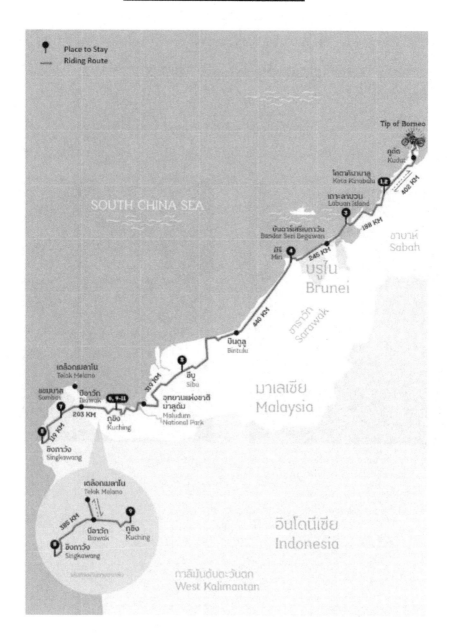

Chapter 4 What Must a Man Do to Win Over a Woman?

Ten days had passed. I had traveled from Chiang Mai to Kota Kinabalu. Upon arriving at the airport, I called a Grab to pick me up right away. Oh, this isn't Thailand. This is Malaysia where Grab isn't illegal.

A while back, Malaysia had both Grab and Uber services, but in 2018 Uber sold its Southeast Asia business to Grab in a multi-billion-dollar deal. The Singaporean government fined both companies totaling over $13 million Singapore dollars for antitrust violations -- because their secret merger would prohibit free market competition.

Ultimately, Uber is now gone and there's only Grab left. Still, it's better than taxis, at least that's how I feel.

I arrived one day before the tour started. So, tonight, I had to pay for my own accommodation and chose to book the same place -- Hotel Shangri-La.

It didn't take long to reach the hotel. But from the looks of it, this place didn't seem to meet the five-star standards of the Shangri-La chain so I checked the official Shangri-La website. I knew it. My suspicions were proven true. There are two Shangri-La hotels in Kota Kinabalu, and this is not one of them. It's a "fake" Shangri-La! -- or as we called in Thai, a "dyed-cat" (translator's note: There is no English equivalent for this Thai expression, but the closest one may be 'turn a sow's ear into a silk purse') Shangri-La!

Tonight, I'll sleep at a "dyed-cat" (fake) Shangri-La. Tomorrow afternoon, I'll get the "undyed" (genuine) Ducati.

Hmmm... Or maybe even the Ducati is a "dyed cat" (fake)? A reputable Italian motorcycle owned by Audi, a German company, but assembled in Rayong, Thailand.

Oh, well. The brochure says that it has eighty-eight horsepower. So, if it does not have eighty-eight "catpower", I'm fine with it.

The next morning, while getting breakfast, I looked for a local newspaper to read, wanting to know what was going on in the city. I stumbled upon a Harley-Davidson elegantly parked in a hardware store. Avid bikers must be like people contracting a deadly virus. It's incurable. Once you see it, you have to own it and flaunt it.

Finally, I found a copy of the Borneo Post newspaper, costing 1.20 Malaysian Ringgit (RM) or about 10 Thai Baht (THB). The headline was about Thai politics -- not too bad at all. Our politics did make an international headline in Borneo. The picture probably sums it up better than my description, on what was written about us.

Next, a woman was sentenced to 17 years in prison and a fine of 39,000 RM or nearly 300,000 THB for drunk driving and causing an accident. Four people were killed and one was disabled. Drunk driving is certainly a major problem in today's world that many countries are faced with.

Then, there was the news about Anwar Ibrahim[3], Mahathir's arch nemesis, who eventually joined forces with Mahathir to overthrow Najib Razak's government. (Overthrowing in their sense, unlike what we've seen in some of their neighboring countries, was achieved by winning the election). Anwar Ibrahim had to declare his assets, just like Thai politicians do. He declared 10.7 million RM, or nearly 80 million THB. The additional assets were from land ownership which appreciates over time. The news did not mention how many watches he owned and if those watches were his or "borrowed"[4].

With the recently-held elections, Malaysian politics had just changed its direction. This marked the first time that the opposition party had won since the formation of Malaysia after gaining its independence.

To make a rough comparison, the former Malaysian government led by Najib Razak was probably similar to the Thaksin government (of Thailand). With progressive thinking, focus on investment, push for the country's development, economic growth through government investment, as well as promotion of investment from China in housing and high-speed train projects, a lot of people might have liked it in the beginning, but not all people felt that way as time passed. Then, the opposition party that had never won before, emerged victorious without needing anybody to "return the happiness[5]" to them.

And similar to India, roughly speaking, its former government led by Prime Minister Manmohan Singh probably shared some characteristics like the Thaksin government as well. He made his way from being Minister of Finance and was good at propelling the country's economy forward by means of capitalism -- the Overseas Citizenship of India (OCI)[6] policy was his idea.   After ten years of Prime Minister Singh's tenure, Mr. Narendra Modi, a rather common man and a former chai wallah, gained victory and formed a government, swinging the political pendulum back to conservative control. There was no need to call on anyone to return the people's happiness either.

This is also the way it is in the United States of America and every country that has free elections. With a good political system, the people's happiness will be returned to them automatically without the need for anyone to return it to them.

After I had finished with the Borneo Post newspaper and breakfast, it was time to visit the museum to learn about the infamous legend of the 'Head Hunters' Their story began simply with an argument between two people from two villages. It was not clear if the dispute was over a woman or because of some bad blood.

When the quarrel was over, one party died, and scuffles between the villages ensued.

Much like in Shakespeare's Romeo and Juliet, the first village, let's suppose that its name was the 'Capulet Village' felt insulted and, with no interest in talking it over, had to reclaim their dignity from the other village. -- let's say its name was 'Montague Village'. Whoever could display more heads on the wall was the 'big gun'. They would reign supreme over all villages, bringing fame to their village and themselves.

Apart from bringing personal pride, such reputation was also a chick magnet. This is a good example that girls always like bad boys since time immemorial. So, if a girl breaks up with some guy from the village by saying, "you're too good for me.", this probably means that that dude has too few heads displayed on his wall, maybe?

And if that dude couldn't forget her, then it was time to hunt for more heads...Brrrr!

Himpunan tengkorak digantung di sebuah rumah di Kampung Hungab, Penampang, Tahun 2000.
(Sumber: Buku "HEAD-HUNTING AND THE MAGANG CEREMONY IN SABAH", 2001 by Peter R. Phelan.)

Chapter 5 It Didn't Take Long for Broken Promises to Emerge

After the museum, I called a 'legal' Grab, to take me to go eat spaghetti. The driver was a plain looking but very charming woman. We had a great conversation. Before this, she lived in a town near Brunei running a small online business on the internet. Her business was going well when she had to move to Kota Kinabalu because of her father's job relocation. Her father is a civil servant and when ordered to transfer, they had to move. After that, her online business suffered because, according to her, Brunei's economy is much better than Kota Kinabalu.

She is very good on the computer. Despite the negative impact on the sales, she doesn't actually need to be a Grab driver. But she said that working alone in front of a computer screen day in and day out can be very boring. Driving allows her to meet and talk to people and doing so helps brighten her days.

So, I continued our conversation on to... of course, the topic of the newly installed government.

"You've got a new prime minister. How is it?"

"Much better than before. As soon as the new government came in, they immediately announced oil price cuts. Corruption has also decreased, but the economy could be better if the government doesn't keep coming up with complicated rules and regulations." Conservative governments tend to complicate matters with complex laws.

After the spaghetti, it was time to go get the eighty-eight "catpower" Ducati - - I, mean, the eighty-eight horsepower Ducati at the port!

There she was, elegantly parked right there -- The most beautiful yellow Ducati that outshone all the bikes on the trip. (This is an objective opinion, totally not biased towards my own bike at all.) After picking her up, I rode a short distance back to the hotel.

In the afternoon when the sun was low, it was time to go for a joy ride and see the city. I didn't invite anyone to come along because I wasn't very well acquainted to anyone in the group. So, I went solo, starting with worshiping the Scripture at a Sikh temple.

The Sikhs in this city originated from the colonial period during the time of colonial British rule. The first Sikhs arrived as police officers. And the beautiful Sikh temples were built shortly thereafter. I spoke with some Sikh people here. They warned me not to ride anywhere alone, and that I should ride together in a group to avoid the danger of bike-jacking.

When I explained that we had a group of more than ten motorcycles taken care of by a tour company, they seemed more relieved. After praying to the Scripture, I took the Ducati on the beach road. Kota Kinabalu is famous for its mountains, but the sea is equally beautiful, and riding along the seashore always feels amazing.

The beautiful city exudes charm and is growing with many new shopping malls, and gorgeous condos, both under construction and completed. The market was bustling just like Chiangmai's 'Kad Luang' (Central Market) where visitors from out of town go to shop. The market was near the sea in the central area of town. There were shoppers who arrived by car and by boat. There must be many islands in the area.

Riding the Ducati abroad gives me more confidence than riding the two-cylinder, melodious, Red Triumph because of the divine eight-piston Brembo brake system. The weather was hot, but not unbearable, making the ride very enjoyable. I rode around and found Kota Kinabalu's signature roundabout.

At the center of the roundabout stood a statue of a Marlin. It was erected to celebrate the city in 2000. Marlins have strong muscles and they can swim a 100-meter distance in 4 seconds at 90 km. per hour. They hold the record for the fastest swimming fish in the world, and with their strong power, they are famous in sport fishing.

Both the marlin and the yellow Ducati are swift and powerful. Though I'm not quite sure if the Ducati can cover 100 meters in 4 seconds, I'm sure that it has more power, with its 88 horsepower, while the marlin only has 1 'fishpower'.

After taking enough photos, I headed back to the hotel.

In the evening, there was a tour briefing session for the next day's trip. I was expecting a good briefing but I was wrong.

"Welcome to Kota Kinabalu." That was the only one best sentence I heard throughout the whole briefing.

"As you all know we had planned to have 200 motorcycles, but only over 70 have registered. Fifty motorcyclists decided to go on the Mongolia trip instead, so there remains 14 of you. As a result, we don't have enough money to hire a service vehicle."

A service vehicle is important to us and it's clearly specified in the tour company's brochure. Many people had not prepared their repair and maintenance equipment because they believed there would be a service vehicle available.

More than ten of us who had just got to know each other could only exchange uneasy glances, probably thinking the same thought, "What on earth made me sign up with this company?"

"Our program needs to be changed. We will cancel the trip to Labuan Island due to .... " And in the end, the tour operator started not to see eye to eye with the team they brought in.

The team was led by Tuan Haji (Tuan means "Mr., Haji is his name") who is truly passionate about motorcycles. He owns a big-ass, white Harley-Davidson with gigantic bat wings covering its round head light. Everyone knows that Harley-Davidson riders are very clear and experienced in life. After a moment of tension, the briefing escalated into a verbal altercation in the hotel's restaurant.

"Are you crazy? What if the motorcycles break down? What do we do?" Tuan Haji spat.

"Don't worry. We already contacted motorcycle repair shops along the route. If there are any problems, the nearest shop will come to offer assistance." The tour company managed to pull off a good and credible answer, always. But when Tuan Haji asked which shops they had contacted... the tour company changed the subject.

Finally, Steve, a Chinese Malaysian who used to work in America as a businessman and an expert in turning around businesses that suffered loss of profit, interrupted, "You go fight among yourselves. What time do we leave tomorrow? We're going to bed." So, the chaotic briefing ended.

Today, I got to ride around town for only 23.8 km. The "dyed-cat" briefing was bogus. The food was bad. The music was no good. Hotel Shangri-La was a fake. It didn't take long for the tour company to break their promises. I went to bed with a hunch that more surprises were definitely waiting for us.

Chapter 6 Truly Asia vs Amazing Thailand

The big picture for this trip is a motorcycle ride from the top of Borneo, aka the Tip of Borneo, which is in the state of Sabah, Malaysia, to Labuan Island by ferry. From there, we board another ferry to Brunei, ride through Brunei to the State of Sarawak, Malaysia, then on to the town Pontianak Indonesia -- a city which is right on the equator.

We will cross the Equator there, then come back to finish the trip in the town of Kuching, the State of Sarawak, Malaysia. Kuching in Bahasa Malaysia means cat. It is said that in days of old this used to be the dwelling place for a great number of wild cats. Currently, the city is decorated with lots of cat motifs. This includes a cat museum which is its top tourist attraction.

Most of the route is on the Asian Highway 150 locally known as the Pan-Borneo Highway[7]. The overall distance is about 2,000 kilometers, which is roughly the equivalent of the distance from the northernmost spot of Siam at Mae Sai to the southernmost tip of Thailand at Betong. The whole trip takes 12 days and 11 nights.

The tour package began at Port Klang near Kuala Lumpur, with the motorcycles being shipped via ferry to Kota Kinabalu in the north of the island. Then, after the trip has ended, the motorcycles will be sent from Kuching, which is in the south of the island back to Port Klang and the trip ends there. On the way going, the motorcycles are on the ferry for about 7days, and 4 days on the way back.

All of the more than ten motorcycles joining this trip came from Malaysia except for the yellow Ducati and her master from Thailand. I don't look very Thai in terms of physical appearance, so I explained that I'm a Thai of Indian descent. I practice the Sikh religion. In other words, I'm a 'Singh'. The word 'Singh' is added to the end of everyone's name in Sikh religion. After I gave that explanation, all the Malaysians understood right away.

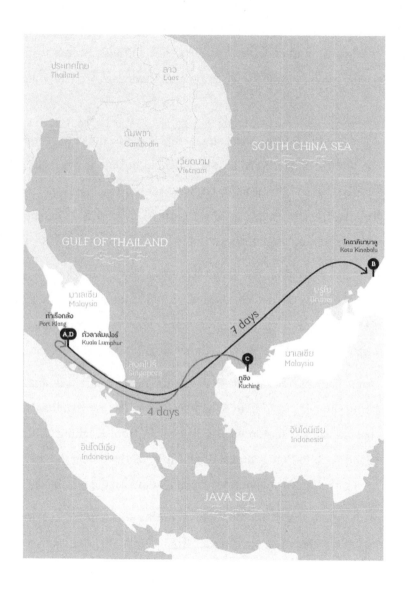

From my observation and my conversation with some Malaysian friends from the past two trips, being born a Malaysian, one has to look at one's lineage. If one is of Indian descent, they would learn an Indian language from childhood to preserve their own cultural identity. Then the children are taught to speak three languages: Indian, Bahasa Malaysia, and English. The person's legal name that appears on an identification document would be an Indian name.

By the same token, if they are of Chinese descent, they will learn Chinese since childhood to preserve their own culture as well, and will be taught to speak three languages – Chinese, Bahasa Malaysia and English, and maintain their real Chinese name which also appears on their ID card and passport.

If they are native Malaysian, or Malay, they will be taught to speak their own language, the Bahasa Malaysia and English, and be treated according to the Bumiputra policy. This, according to some, breeds inequality. I couldn't really understand the true sentiment of Malaysian people toward the Bumiputra policy. From my conversation, some didn't care, but others showed their discontent. This would come out after we got to know each other for a bit. But all in all, no matter what religion, or ethnicity, they grow up in a classroom of diversity -- with all the languages, all the religions, and all the differences. That's why Malaysians can preserve their heritage so well, while having a good understanding of their compatriots' diverse cultures.

As I see it, this is an authentic "Truly Asia[8]" mix.

But their view of us ... Vincent, a tall and thin Chinese Malaysian man, owner of the BMW GS800, said, "I think that your country has more unity and harmony than my country because they have assimilated everybody into Thai."

Thais of Indian descent, or Thais of Chinese descent in Thailand have Thai names on their national ID cards. Everyone speaks Thai. (And most speak broken English). They are all Thais and not considered that much different.

I agree. This is a good viewpoint that I never had perceived before. While they (Malaysians) have a good "Truly Asia" blend, we have a Pad Thai style, Amazing Thailand[9] model.

Then came the departure date. Tuan Haji managed to get a service car to drive behind us. under a cloud of an extremely tense atmosphere. This was the first day we would get to ride seriously in Borneo. Today's route would partially span the Pan Borneo Highway, then exit to a small local road heading to the Tip of Borneo or the northernmost spot of Borneo. We would stop to gas up at Kudat and return to the same "dyed-cat (fake)" Shangri-La Hotel.

The roundtrip distance would be around 365 kilometers. I didn't know the condition of the road, nor the way local people drive. The tour company's briefing the night before did not mention anything about the rules, tips, or even safety precautions of riding.

Before leaving, we huddled together to pray...

In Sikhism, before embarking on anything, we pray for blessings from our gods as well. I was very glad during the prayer. All of us, Muslims and non-Muslims, Malay, Chinese, British (there was one Caucasian), and Thai-Sikh, stood together praying for the blessings from Allah with a united soul. We had all come together because of our love of the open road and the extension of our souls, called 'motorcycles'.

Chapter 7 Riding on the Pan Borneo Highway

The prayer for blessing ended with "Ameen" which is similar to "Amen".

All the students of Prince Royal College (in Chiang Mai) in my batch had gone to church and prayed for God's blessing that always ended with "Amen". This reminded me of the past.

I was wearing shorts and riding a top-of-the-line motorcycle. According to one famous Thai novelist, top-of-the-line model is the best, the superlative, the ultimate motorcycle of the production line.

In those days, it was the Honda NSR150 -- a two-stroke, 150cc, motorcycle, with a single shock absorber, front and rear disc brakes, water-cooled engine, thirty-one horsepower, and weighing a little bit over hundred kilograms. All this came with a top speed that I never attained.

A single word of "Amen" was enough to take me that far back and brought such a great feeling and a smile to my face. It was a special connection forged between a Sikh boy and Jesus Christ.

And this was my first time praying with Muslims to ask for Allah's blessings to grant safe passage to all the motorcycles lovers. This could be called my first connection with Allah.

And then it was time to start the engine.

With a single press of the "start" button, the Ducati was blowing smoke from the rear pair of exhaust pipes. Even after seven days on the ferry, she showed no sign of lethargy or idleness. If anything, there was only the readiness to dash forward. As soon as the peg-patterned, Pirelli tires of the raspy, yellow Ducati started to turn, her master had to grapple with the first thing -- the 'roundabouts'.

Because this place was once a British colony, there are tons of roundabouts and no traffic lights on the roads. The size of the roundabouts varies depending on the size and number of cars in that area. Small intersections, small roundabouts, not a problem. The problem was with the big intersections, big roundabouts, the right of way, the speed and the right moment to enter the roundabout was something new that needed to promptly be learned.

The rule here is that the vehicles in the roundabout have the right of way. In fact, Thailand's law is the same. But in practice, if it were a straight road, a lot of times the vehicles in the roundabout stopped for you. Also, we have fewer roundabouts and most of them are small.

Here, vehicles in the roundabout clearly have the right of way and everybody normally follows that rule. This was new to me and I had to learn, starting with the humongous roundabout outside the hotel. I had to dash without hesitation as soon as there was some space behind the vehicle in the roundabout. If I went too fast, there

would be no time to make the curve of the roundabout and I could crash and embarrass myself in front of my friends. On the other hand, if I went too slow and cut in front of the oncoming vehicle in the roundabout, I'd be called names and embarrass my fellow riders with the Thai license plates.

After my baptism of fire on how to enter and exit the roundabouts, we eventually managed to get out of town successfully. The sight-seeing ride out of town and refreshing morning air felt great and it got better as we entered the Pan-Borneo Highway.

The surroundings looked very much like the North of Thailand, resembling the most beautiful, and the greatest place to live with the name that stays forever young -- 'Chiang Mai' (it literally translates as 'New City'), only at a larger scale. Mountains got much bigger, and fully covered with foliage. Though I saw something about forest encroachment in the paper the other day, I didn't notice any denuded mountains like those in my home country throughout the trip.

The trees along both sides of the road were very tall. The sky was bright because the Pan Borneo Highway runs parallel to the coast almost all the way. Although the sea was hardly visible, the scenery was absolutely beautiful. All the curves and not too many cars made the ride very pleasant and enjoyable on a five out of five scale all the way.

In Thailand, when passing villages, we see the golden glow of temples, the sanctuary for discovery of life's true meaning, the immortality of Siddhartha's preaching, that brings peace and familiarity. But in Malaysia, when we pass any village, the beauty of qabbas (domes) of mosques gave me the sense of love and faith in Allah, reflecting the life goals of Muslims -- "to love and serve God".

The whole day was spent on the motorcycles amidst splendid natural surroundings. The natural rain forest on Borneo was lush. Big trees spread their canopies on high mountains. Smoothly paved road curves its way caressing the scenic greeneries just like the rave review.

The travelers on this trip are from a mix of faiths from Islam, Christianity, Buddhism to Sikhism. Apart from each person's adherence to his own religion, we were bound together by the love of riding motorcycles. Everyone was generous and helped take care of each other along the way. We ate together, laughed together, signaled to each other, waited to ride together, and be happy together.

On the first day, we covered a distance of 401.6 kilometers. What I felt today was that God loves and blesses everyone regardless of class, race, or religion -- unlike in any news we read in the newspaper, unlike what President Trump and his CIA team tried to tell us, and unlike the news we see on television about all the strife and unrest.

There was no other feeling beside friendship, love, and a unified spirit on a motorcycle. ... in this beautiful country of Allah's.

Chapter 8 An Expedition Just for Fun

Today was the third day of our trip. But before we get to the story about the trip, let me go back to the briefing we had the night before -- the briefing that I had expected to be helpful but I was wrong. The tour company wanted to cancel the trip to Labuan Island for the reason that we guessed, which was to make the most profit.

Also, the new route that was proposed to us at the briefing was not done in a professional manner at all. It looked so poorly prepared that we could not help but think if they even knew how to use Google Maps. They proposed that we ride to Miri via the Pan Borneo Highway all the way through Brunei for a distance of over 400 kilometers and then spend one day sightseeing in Miri. The proposed distance looked good -- not too much, not too little -- in the northern Thai dialect, we call this 'Mok Muan' or 'Just for Fun'.

While everyone was getting ready to go to bed, Tuan Haji didn't want what they proposed and neither did the Indian-Thai of Sikh religion. As a local person Tuan Haji knew what covering 400 kilometers on the next day meant. I too had done my homework, and I also knew what Tuan Haji was talking about.

The Pan Borneo Highway was under construction for width expansion -- almost the whole stretch of its 2,000 kilometers. Some parts had been finished, and some were still under construction. Many stretches of the road are like a struggle between the 'gigantic mountains', God's engineering projects, and 'tiny human beings' with enough engineering knowledge to somewhat outwit the sea and the mountains.

The fierce struggle was ongoing and many parts of the road were muddy and if it rained, we would run into a motherlode of muddy conditions. And that was only part of the problem.

If you look at the map, you'll see that Brunei is a small country, on the edge of Borneo. But if you look carefully, Brunei is quite special -- it is divided into two disconnected parts.

If you didn't zoom in closely, you'd think that it is in one piece. Once you zoom in, you'll notice that the two parts are disconnected. And you will see further that the Pan Borneo Highway will take us from Sabah to Sarawak. Even though both states are in Malaysia, to cross the border, you would need to get your passport stamped. These people are what I call 'Indie Malaysia' –this is to be explained later.

From Sarawak to Brunei, from Brunei to return to Sarawak, and from there, this road would take us from Sarawak back to Brunei again. Then, after running parallel to the beach for a while, it would leave Brunei back to Sarawak again before entering Miri. That means we would have to go through immigration and get our passports stamped for a total of ten times in one day. If we combine bad road conditions, the rain, and ten times of going through customs in a single day, we are not likely to accomplish all of this before sunset.

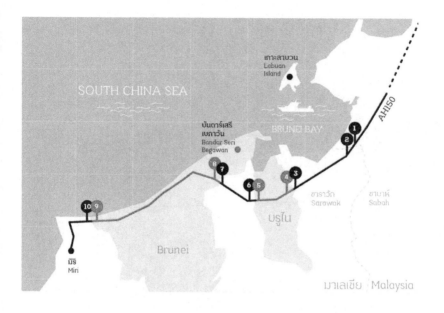

Who would want to ride on the road where human engineering works are combatting fiercely with God's engineering on a rainy night? The discussion then escalated further into an argument, and the tour company asked Tuan Haji to leave the room. In fact, to say that he was kicked out is probably more accurate.

Tuan Haji is a stocky guy who rides a big-ass, white Harley-Davidson with batwing fairing, and he's from Brunei. He shouted sharply while pointing his finger toward the tour company, "Never in my over 60 years of living have I ever been asked to leave a meeting room before." Then, he stormed out of the meeting room, looking extreme upset.

I began to argue in the politest way I could, "We should go to Labuan Island to avoid racing against time. And from my research, it is a special island. Please reconsider." It was politeness, mixed with decisiveness, combined with rays of evil that I learned from Nusara.

In the end, the meeting was adjourned. Steve, a tall and well-built, Chinese Malaysian businessman who owns an 800cc, inline-triple-engine Triumph motorcycle, concluded that "You guys go and discuss among yourselves, but we must do everything as advertised and we're going to Labuan."

I went up to bed at the 'dyed-cat' aka fake Shangri-La and almost didn't get any sleep all night because of diarrhea ... If I remember correctly, I got up to go to the bathroom six times.

On the morning of the third day, we were heading to Labuan Island. Tuan Haji disappeared. There was no service vehicle behind us. Only Alex, who claimed to be a friend of the tour company, was escorting us to the ferry pier, about 140 kilometers from the hotel. No formation was arranged. No vehicle behind us, nothing. It was completely different from the advertisement in the brochure. (See an explanation about group riding at the end of the Chapter).

The Pan Borneo Highway today was quite unlike what it was yesterday. Although the surroundings were as beautiful, the road condition was not the same. The road was under construction, so we had to zigzag and keep dodging potholes almost all the way until we exited to a small local road that ran along the beach. Only then, did we get to ride in a more relaxing manner, and started to enjoy the scenery along the road.

Finally, we arrived at the ferry terminal and had to wait for almost three hours to get on board. Then we spent almost two hours on the ferry surrounded by beautiful, yet unfamiliar scenery. At long last, we reached Labuan Island at about half past two. The weather was extremely hot. The badass, yellow Ducati, became a hot barbecue grill for her master's calves again.

Hot ... but I still love her.

Motorcycle Group Riding

The Motorcycle Safety Foundation (www.msf-usa.org) is an agency that works to improve motorcyclists' safety through research, education, and training. The education and training, in particular, is to encourage lifelong learning in motorcyclists. The agency is also responsible for the development of a certification program for motorcycle coaches. It also cooperates with the government in safety research, promotion of public awareness and governmental-support driver's license training. The agency is a non-profit organization and receives support from BMW, BRP, Harley Davidson, Honda, Indian Motorcycle, Kawasaki, KTM, Suzuki, Triumph and Yamaha.

The agency provides driving instructions for formation riding as follows: The formation of a procession should focus mainly on the enjoyment and safety of the ride.

Arrive prepared: Arrive on time with a full tank of gas.

Join a riders' meeting: Discuss the route, rest and fuel stops, and hand signals to be used during the trip. Assign a lead (sometimes called marshal, lead bike, or lead rider), and sweep (sometimes called sweeper, tail bike or tail rider) riders. Both should be experienced riders who are well-versed in group riding procedures. The leader should be aware of each rider's skill level before the ride and monitor the riders during the ride.

Manageable size: ideally five to seven riders. If there are more riders, break the group into smaller sub-groups, each with a lead and sweep rider.

Ride prepared: At least one rider in each group should have a first-aid kit and full tool kit, and all riders should carry a cell phone, so the group is prepared for any problem that they might encounter.

Ride in formation: The staggered riding formation allows a proper space cushion between motorcycles so that each rider has enough time and space to maneuver and to react to hazards. A minimum of 2-second following distance is recommended and more is preferred on a curvy road, poor road surfaces, or entering/leaving highways.

Further recommendations on riding in formation can be found at https://www.msf-usa.org/downloads/group_ride.pdf.

Chapter 9 The Feet with a Harley-Davidson Attitude

After we had finally dragged ourselves safely to the hotel, I proposed to the group that we should go for a ride around Labuan Island in the late afternoon. Everyone agreed. We set the time to meet and went to take a shower and rest.

Compared to my beloved Chiang Mai, riding around Labuan Island was like completing the third ring road (Route 121) beginning at the Seven Hundred Years Stadium, running along the canal road, entering the third ring road, and ending at the same place. The distance of about 50 kilometers is excellent, and we were confident that it would be a great ride. When the sun was low, we prepared to leave, by arranging our own formation, and planning our own route. Then we headed out of the hotel with a tour company staff in a van following us as the end car.

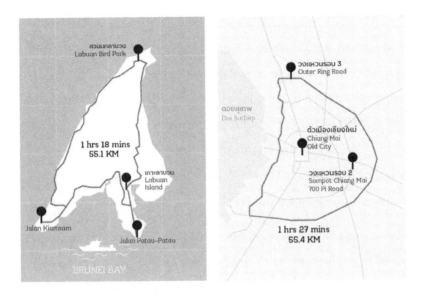

But it was not God's will. And everyone knows that if God is not willing, who could stand in His way?

God sent us three of the 1% ERs (for the description of 1% ERs, please see the end of the chapter). Everyone knows that those who like to ride Harley-Davidsons have an extraordinary lifestyle. They are truly the 1% ERs. They have a strong personality and when dissatisfied with anything, they don't want to be contradicted. They are overly confident in their own potential, their own attitude, and their own feet.

Three Harley-Davidsons appeared in front of the hotel, looking irritated. Before we could be startled or ask any questions, those three signaled with hand gestures telling us begrudgingly to follow. Though more than ten of us wanted a sightseeing ride to take in the exhilarating experience of riding around the Labuan Island, we weren't sure that our feet, despite the bigger number, would be a match for those fewer feet but full of attitude of Harley-Davidson's.

All we could do was to follow ...

I had been to many islands -- Koh Si Chang, Koh Kood, Koh Samet, or some other islands where I went with my motorcycle, like Koh Lanta, Singapore Island, Penang Island, Phuket Island, but none of them was like Labuan. Malaysia consists of 13 states and 3 federal territories. Labuan is one of the three federal territories with an area of approximately 91 square kilometers -- close to Koh Kood that is approximately 111 square kilometers in size. However, the population of Koh Kood is around 2,500, while Labuan's a little bit under 100,000.

Most islands have two economic machines: fishing and tourism. Penang has one additional one which is the business sector, while Singapore has an additional financial sector making a total of four machines. But Labuan is different. Labuan has only one economic machine. It is a colossal one.

The three guys took us riding for a while, then they took a turn into an alley where about 20 magnificent Harley-Davidsons with its riders brimming with similar attitudes were waiting. The motorcycles revved their signature roars through their powerful exhaust pipes as we arrived. This startled us quite a bit.

SARAWAK BORNEO CROSS COUNTRY RALLY 2019 DAY 03 PART 2 SUNSET WITH H O G LABUAN

Surprise to us that H.O.G. of Labuan are waiting for us at Dato Harris residence

0:32 / 7:11

Right after the last bike turned in, the alley was blocked by the Harley-Davidson that was waiting at the entrance of the alley. Immediately, he glowered at the van. Tension was rising. The van driver, Bob, appeared to understand what was going on, but the tour company didn't. He opened the van door and walked out, probably hoping to talk to the group leader.

The atmosphere got even more intense to the breaking point. We confessed later that we really didn't know what was going to happen next and were all scared. Finally, the tour company was ordered away sternly by about 1% of ER Harley-Davidsons of Labuan Island, "Go back and stay in the hotel."

After the tour company left, the 1% ER Harley-Davidsons set out and signaled to us to follow. All we could do was to follow each other and try to look as cute and charming as possible knowing full well about the number and potential as well as the attitude of each of these feet. We were at a disadvantage.

What is 1% ER?

In the early days of motorcycle commercial production, motorcycle clubs did not yet wreak havoc, or were viewed as outlaws. They were more like road trip buddies, because the motorcycle speed did not much surpass that of a bicycle.

Then, during the World War I era, motorcycle performance had greatly improved, and even more so during World War II. Consequently, this marked a turning point for motorcycle clubs.

This turning point saw motorcycle clubs turning into motorcycle gangs, and hence the rise of countercultures.

Some people concluded that this turning point came from the Americans who had gone to war. They saw death right before their eyes, and therefore wanted to live freely and no longer cared for any rules or restrictions in their life -- including speed limits or legal restrictions. They survived the war and wanted to revolt.

Some said that the Americans who returned from war were addicted to the adrenaline rush from what went on in the battlefield. This caused them to constantly need a rush from risky and adventurous activities. Breaking the rules or rebelling gave them that adrenaline rush.

While most people who got married, bought a house, for want of a peaceful life after returning from the war marked the beginning of a Baby Boomers era, some looked at mortgages and marriage, as clearly the opposite of freedom. Moreover, America did not suffer much after the end of World War II. The economy flourished. Tremendous numbers of roads were built to connect all the states. Motorcycles with big engines were affordable, and the experience of riding a motorcycle on a smooth, long road was a great new experience and easily attainable. Riding on the highway was a true freedom.

July 1947 was a major turning point. At an event organized by the American Motorcyclist Association (AMA), which had been held regularly for 10 years prior, in a small town in California, members and their motorcycles came to have a good time together. But that year, some people felt that they didn't have enough fun.

According to Life Magazine, some members of the Pissed Off Bastards Motorcycle Club added more fun by racing their motorcycles on the streets through traffic lights and also smashing glass windows, destroying shops and occupying that small town.

The Police came to the rescue and arrested many motorcyclists who had more fun than others. Most were as drunk as a skunk. It was then that the world got to see the image of the outlaw motorcycle gangs in revolt.

And after that incident, the president of AMA condemned these groups through the media that 99% of the motorcycle clubs are good, only 1% are outlaw motorcycle gangs, hence, the 1% rebels (The One Percenter).

In 1948, one year after the incident, the excessively fun-loving members of the Pissed Off Bastards Motorcycle Club thought that the revolting 1% was the ultimate lifestyle. It was the very definition of the word 'rebel'. I am the 1%. I'm remarkable. I am not the remaining 99%. So, they decided to break from the Pissed Off Bastards Motorcycle Club and founded a 1% rebellious motorcycle club under the name 'the Hells Angels', that has become the symbol of the rebellious counterculture of American motorcyclists to this day.

This was the origin of the 1% ER symbol on the jacket. It came from the AMA's condemnation and the admiration of the condemnation by the rebels.

Let's take a look at some of the important events of the Hells Angels. In 1963, the Hells Angels rode into one town and did whatever they wanted there. A year later, four members of the rebellious Hells Angels were charged with statutory rape. Though the rape case was dismissed the following year, it was clear how anarchistic the 1%ER Hells Angels were in the eyes of the general public.

Then came the historic event that would forever be remembered... It was the 1969 event at the Rolling Stone concert, where the Hells Angels were invited by the Rolling Stone to be their bodyguards!! It was the perfect recipe for disaster.

And disaster struck indeed, when a gunshot was heard, one outlaw Hells Angels performed his duty perfectly by putting a knife into the guy who fired the gun almost instantly, grabbed the gun from his hand and dragged the guy away before more people beat him. The camera did a great job by capturing almost everything, and the glorious Hells Angels guard had to go to court for murder charge.

It was definitely a murder case, but the Hells Angels guy didn't like the existence of the law. He rebelled against the law. He didn't say that it was self-defense, or *force majeure*, or whatever was the legal term. He was a rebellious 1% ER ... He replied clearly, true to the outlaw style, that the guy drew a gun, so I stuck a knife in him. Everything was justified ...

And this has been the way of 1% ERs.

Chapter 10 Sunset on Labuan Beach

All of our over ten motorcycles were surrounded by the gigantic Harley-Davidsons that were bellowing their earth-shattering sound. Straddling over them were their riders with sharp features hiding cryptic attitudes. There were a lead and tail Harley-Davidsons for the whole caravan and those who blocked the traffic at each intersection to let us pass. The facial expression and body language of 1% ERs appeared friendlier. They were giving us fingers -- not the middle one but the thumb followed by a smile on their face. The charged atmosphere became more relaxing.

The road was beautiful and smooth in the setting sun. We saw people jogging on the side of the road, sitting on the beach. We rode past a university that looked well-groomed and well-built.

Lacking, were serious looking drivers fighting traffic jams like in Phuket, or those that tailgate you to death and in an extreme hurry like in Penang. We found relaxed drivers and people. Everyone looked laid-back. There were no foreign tourists on the road, or in places that we rode pass or by the beach.

The Harley-Davidson gang brought us to a spot near the beach. After we had finished parking, we went down to chat. Everyone appeared friendly and welcoming with a cordial look in their eyes expressing the love of the two-wheeler lifestyle.

The group leader was called 'Harris', a native of Labuan. He had been appointed a Dato[10] , so we called him Dato Harris. I heard that he owns some old rigs and is very wealthy. Whether or not this is true, I do not know.

He told us that "We received word from the tour company that there would be a group of motorcyclists traveling to our island. We are very happy and have prepared a warm welcome. But at the last minute, we were notified by the tour company that you said that you didn't care to come to Labuan anymore. We felt bad to hear that."

We were utterly shocked. Motorcycle lovers like us didn't want to come to Labuan Island? This must be crazy! It was absolutely not true.

At a meeting last night, the tour company told us that the trip to Labuan was canceled -- the brochure clearly states that the program can be modified without prior notice.

Dato Harris continued, "We have a beautiful island, friendly and easygoing people. A lot of motorcycle groups always want to visit. The groups that came here in the past received a warm welcome from us. Some groups who had little time even parked their motorcycle in a nearby town and took the plane here."

The host explained further that "At first, we misunderstood you, but one of our group members said that what the tour company said was not true. The truth is that the tour company did not want to bring you here because they wanted to save on the cost of the ferry."

There are no secrets in the world ... And right then, the white Harley-Davidson with a giant batwing fairing turned in toward where we were parked.

An over-sixty-year-old stocky man with an absolute passion for motorcycle riding by the name of 'Tuan Haji' emerged. They belonged to the same group.

Besides so much love of a two-wheeler lifestyle that he taught his three children to follow his footsteps, this group leader also had an undying love for Labuan Island. What the tour company did deliberately caused Labuan Island to lose the opportunity to show off its beauty to us. He was upset and decided to kidnap us from the tour company and to show us some good experience in Labuan.

"We heard that you had planned to ride around the island, but we would like to present the sunset by the sea on the Labuan beach instead. We are confident that you will be pleased with such beauty." Dato Harris said with pride. "Everyone on Labuan Island is doing business related to the oil and natural gas industry, one way or another. Our city runs slowly, smoothly, and is very nice to live in." I also observed that the members of this group seemed calm, relaxed and enjoying life.

Glancing at the sea of rolling waves that softly glittered in the setting sun, I didn't see any fishing boats, but large ocean-goers, tankers for oil and gas, and of course, oil platforms, some of which were visible in the line of sight.

At this time, all the hostile feelings had dissipated and substituted by the friendliness and camaraderie among the lovers of two-wheeled spiritual charms. We talked, laughed, took pictures together happily. And when the sun was setting, all of us savored the golden reflection of the last rays on the beach and the beautiful sea. It was as impressive as Dato Harris had promised.

The romantic ambiance made me miss Nusara right then and there, so I called her up. "The sun is about to set over the sea. I'm overwhelmed by such beauty that it made me miss you."

Nusara might begin to need me back closer to her, but she probably understood the reason why I came this far away. It wasn't my desire to come, but only to please her.

"Go away." Nusara answered curtly.

'A woman who has been pleased by a man since bygone days knows no bounds to her own satisfaction.'

The Federation Territory of Labuan or Labuan Island has only one economic machine that is the oil and gas industry.

This highly valued business coexists with the beautiful nature of the sea and has become a special value-added component to the mix, unseen anywhere else. The mixing of a slow life with big business, when seen with my own eyes, felt strangely beautiful, and pleasing to my soul.

Thank God for bringing me here ...

I continued to watch the sun go down with my friends who have extraordinary lifestyles, until the last soft rays vanished. The sea that had just twinkled in the sunset changed to reflect the dazzling glow from the top of the oil rigs.

Chapter 11 A Sea of Bank Notes Wrapped Around the Waves

There is a Sikh temple on Labuan Island. One of my friends in the group saw it from our hotel's window and when we searched Google Map, we found that it was only a few hundred meters away.

It is not uncommon for a Malaysian person to be able to distinguish Sikh temples, from mosques, Buddhist temples, or churches only by viewing its roof. He understands the cultural differences very well.

This morning, I started the day a little earlier than usual by going to ask for blessings from the Scripture at the temple. Two friends accompanied me; Vincent, a Chinese Malaysian and owner of the BMW GS800, and Fu, another Chinese Malaysian, who has been riding his air-cooled boxer engine BMW R1150GS around Thailand until he could communicate fluently in Thai.

We asked for the Scripture's blessings for a fun-filled, safe and happy journey. Then we came back to the hotel and formed up a caravan with our friends and set out.

Day four of the trip. Today's schedule was to depart from Labuan Federation or Labuan Island by ferry to Brunei. After that, we would go from Brunei to Miri in the state of Sarawak, Malaysia. A full page of my passport should be filled with chops today.

We left the hotel a little early, so we had some time to roam around the city. We rode past the central stadium, the harbor, banks, government buildings. The island was clean, beautiful, charming, and had a unique feel to it. It also is a duty-free island. People can trade freely here. The city center had a large, modern hotel about ten storeys high, which had been open since the postwar period and a good display of the island's prosperity. Just that this hotel had a bit of a problem ... It was closed down in 1997 and became abandoned since then. The hotel that used to be a demonstration of the city's wealth has become a gigantic ghost structure across from the town square, causing the island to look quite bad.

We parked and took a group photo with the Labuan sign with a heart around it for keepsake. Then it was time to head to the pier. We intended to get there two hours before the boat leaves to make sure we got on it. We stopped to refill our tank. Gas was included in the tour package, but the tour agent was nowhere to be found.

It didn't matter. We filled it, we paid for it.

Upon arriving at the pier, being motorcyclists coupled with Tuan Haji's popularity put us in front of the line and ensured our spots on the ferry. Then we went to find something to eat nearby. While we were eating, a beggar approached us and asked for some money. I sat next to Tuan Haji, so, he told me that, "In Brunei, our King (Sultan) does not allow beggars. Homeless children living on the roadside will be taken to school, given shelter, and enjoy a good future." He was truly proud of the absolute monarchy system.

And of course, he was still not satisfied with the tour company. "They are all gone today." Tuan Haji continued with a strong facial expression. "I've prepared a warm welcome for them in Brunei."

Nobody would want to be greeted with such an attitude for sure.

After a while, the tour company sent us a message, "I will go ahead to wait for everyone in Miri, to prepare a good hotel and great restaurant to welcome you. This morning, I hurried to travel here by plane." After being chased by the Labuan locals back to the hotel yesterday, they must have guessed what was in store for them. So, there was only Bob, the driver of the van that followed us to the pier. After reading the message, Tuan Haji said it was too bad.

We were the first group to board the ferry. Although it looked like the one we were on to get to Labuan the day before, this one had a much better service, visibly cleaner and the operations more professional. Every motorcycle was fastened with a rope and hooked down to the floor firmly. The bad-ass and dandy, yellow Ducati seemed relaxed and ready for her sea-going voyage.

The weather today was overcast, cool, cloudy but there was no rain. The ferry left the pier on time. It was the perfect weather to hang out on the deck and look around at the unfamiliar vista. The sea here is an industrial ground like what I saw from the beach in Labuan. There are many oil rigs. The businesses in Labuan Island that support these rigs must be doing well.

So many boats were passing us, front, back, left, right. We hardly saw any tourist boats, but container ships and tankers transporting oil and gas. It was beautiful just like seeing bank notes wrapping around the crests of the waves and glittering all over.

The ferry swiftly carried all the powerful motorcycles directly into the Gulf of Brunei -- the land that is clean, beautiful, and ruled by absolute monarchy. We passed by the formidable navy, beautiful buildings and long trans-bay bridges.

Brunei is a small but very rich country. The Sultan of Brunei once was the richest man in the world until Bill Gates defeated him in 1990. He lives an interesting lifestyle. For example, he held a private concert by inviting Bon Jovi, Elton John, Diana Ross, Stevie Wonder to perform in Brunei. Once he also invited Whitney Houston and after the concert, gave her a blank check, saying, "Just write the sum you see fit." She wrote down seven million dollars.

In addition, the vehicles in his possession are what we, the lovers of the open road, all envy. He owns about five thousand of all models, ranging from super cars to luxury cars -- in other words, the motherlode of super cars and luxury cars.

His estimated income is moderate -- a mere 100USD per second, that's all.

Chapter 12 A Genteel Ride in Bandar Seri Begawan

The ferry docked gracefully, and gently. We rode our motorcycles off the ferry and onto the concrete pavement of Brunei, then straight to the customs checkpoint for vehicle inspection. The inspection was efficient. In the morning, we got the document with a barcode on it. All we had to do was scan the document at the laser-scanner. There were no customs officers on duty. The process only took five minutes. Getting through customs for us took a little more time. In just a few minutes we had legally entered Brunei.

Tuan Haji led us to a restaurant in Bandar Seri Begawan via a four-lane coastal highway. The pavement was perfectly smooth with railings along the road. Bright lights shone on every square inch -- perfectly beautiful. If we were to call the E1 highway in West Malaysia from Sadao Toll Plaza to Kuala Lumpur a business-class highway, this would be, without a doubt, a first-class highway.

We felt relaxed and were one with our motorcycles on Brunei's first-class highway. The love of motorcycles bonded us adventure seekers of different faiths and nationalities together in the spirit of friendship and camaraderie. We were happy with the great and professional care we received. Tuan Haji had a thorough understanding about the motorcycle culture. When he got back to his own turf without the tour company bothering him, he was visibly energetic and cheerful.

Tuan Haji blasted the music so loud, everyone could hear it over the first-class Highway. And while putting his bike on cruise-control, he waved both arms in the air, sang along so loudly, and couldn't care less what anybody thought. The gigantic Harley cruised along the highway, delightfully swooshing through the wind. Its enormous, two-cylinder piston V-twin engines generated a powerful, unique sound of Harley-Davidson to accompany the music.

He didn't care about anyone.

https://www.youtube.com/watch?v=x19bqrALcSM&t=469s
SARAWAK BORNEO CROSS COUNTRY RALLY 2019 DAY 04 LABUAN BRUNEI MIRI
– Than Hock Ying channel

The laws here are sacred and work differently from my country. Public consumption of alcohol, taking a woman who is not your wife or relative out, and celebrating Christmas in public are all illegal. All the BMWs acted in a restrained and orderly fashion that even the sound from the bad-ass Ducati's twin exhaust pipes seemed to be softer.

Only the local head honcho Harley-Davidson was frolicking and carefree in his own turf.

I inhaled my lunch because I wanted to try the coffee in Brunei. I wanted to know if the hipster coffee culture had made it across the border and transcended the difference of ruling systems into this country of absolute monarchy.

I searched Google and found an interesting cafe just a few hundred meters away. The name was Roasted Sip, simply meaning "roast and sip". The name gave a feeling of well-roasted coffee ready for people to come in and sip it. In the coffee shop, I found a familiar atmosphere decorated by coffee lovers. The rich coffee aroma lingered in the air. The interior designed for tranquility and comfort invited you to indulge in the flavorful coffee on the menu that's similar around the world.

I hadn't exchanged any Bruneian currency thinking it wasn't necessary. I imagined that a small country surrounded by Malaysia, would accept Malaysian money, but I was wrong. They only accepted Brunei, Singapore and US dollars, none of which I had. It had been a few days since I drank good coffee. No matter what, today I had to do it.

Then I saw a credit card machine, and asked, "Do you accept Visa cards?"

"Yes."

"I'm going to order one cup of coffee. Can I pay with a Visa card? "

"Yes."

The sound of the dark red espresso machine started to brew. The energetic barista gracefully made a hot Americano with elegant moves -- a lifestyle of coffee aficionados. Steam swirled around, emitting fragrant coffee aroma.

Time for a sip... While savoring, I was reminded of Buon Ma Thuat in Vietnam whose coffee culture yielded a familiar taste.

The taste admired by coffee enthusiasts.

The taste that flows through the internet to those who are ready to sell their soul to coffee.

The taste that Carlsberg used to call 'the one taste around the world'.

After getting caffeine into my system, we headed to Istana Nurul Iman, the Sultan of Brunei's royal palace. The palace website explained that it has a hall that can accommodate up to five thousand invited guests of the Sultan.

With an area of two hundred thousand square meters, it has been crowned the largest palace in the world by the Guinness World Records. The Sultan's Palace should be able to host us and our motorcycles easily, but unfortunately, we had an important appointment and couldn't have tea in this reception hall as large as Central Festival, a hyper mall back home.

We had a tea appointment at the Malaysian consulate hosted by the Malaysian ambassador to Brunei.

Chapter 13 Riding on the First-Class Highway

Palan was a Muslim man who was about to graduate from being a father to a grandfather. He looked too young to be a grandfather, maybe because of all the time he spends riding a motorcycle.

He rode a 1200cc, two-cylinder, liquid-cooled but looked air-cooled, Triumph Bonneville T120 with a round headlight, fuel-injection that looks like carburetor, and ride-by-wire accelerator. Ride modes can be adjusted according to weather and road conditions, complete with increased safety with traction control and ABS brakes. Palan's motorcycle had a beautiful, classic silhouette. Its vintage design is like those from the 1980s but its technology is super modern.

Palan was the Ambassador's former classmate, so we had a chance to visit the Malaysian Embassy in Brunei.

When we met the ambassador, everyone shook hands and placed their left hand over their chest. I guess it was like a greeting from the heart that junior people would do toward more senior people -- be it in status or age.

When it was my turn, I performed the gesture as a sign of respect to his culture, and followed by a "wai" or putting my hands together in prayer position while saying "Sawasdee" or "Hello" in Thai. My friends told Mr. Ambassador that Raj is Thai-Sikh. He smiled warmly in response to my goodwill.

An hour and a half passed by. I teased my Malaysian friends that "You guys must love your country so much. We rode across your country for four hours, but we've been sitting in your embassy for an hour and a half now. Don't you want to see Brunei a little?" And everyone laughed happily. And then we took a group picture outside.

Huawei phones have very good cameras. Every evening when we arrived at the hotel, I would send the pictures from my mobile phone to all my friends on WhatsApp group. After three or four days when there were important pictures, my Huawei phone got called to service all the time. Some people named it "Muay Thai phone"

Some called it "Tom Yam Kung phone". In fact, this was only because we were with the ambassador, but when we were among ourselves, some would call it the "Happy Ending Phone" or the "Thai Massage Phone" based on our country's infamous reputation.

After taking the picture, it was time to leave. It was almost five o'clock and we still had about 160 kilometers to go and two more passport stamps. Many people in the group didn't want to ride at night.

"The highway in Brunei has bright lights along the way. We can ride comfortably, nothing to worry about." Tuan Haji remained confident in the superiority of Brunei's highways. What he said was true. The lights covered every square inch of the highway. The road signs were all clearly visible and the traffic lights were first class as well.

The traffic lights in Brunei were first class, both in and outside of the city. I judged them by observing the period when the light almost turned from green to red. There would be no cars ahead and by nature, I usually approached at high speed to see if I could push my luck.

If the light turned red immediately, it would be called 'uneducated' and merciless.

If the light turns yellow then red, this type of traffic light is called Economy Class -- good to have but not good enough to deserve praise.

If the green light flashed with count-down time in seconds, then changed to yellow also with a countdown, this was classified as a business-class traffic light -- It's convenient and makes motorcyclists feel good and they can make precise decision.

If there was a warning light about tens of meters before the traffic light letting us know that the light was about to turn red so we had time to slow down and prepare to brake without fear that others would rear end us, this was the first-class traffic light. It was designed to totally honor motorists just like flight attendants kneeling down to serve you tea on the upper deck of the Airbus A380. The traffic lights in Brunei are the latter --so even though the highway has traffic lights, they are definitely still first class.

We left the Malaysian consulate and headed to Miri. The distance in Brunei was about 130 kilometers on the impressive first-class highway. The yellow Ducati leapt forward at a base speed of 150 kilometers per hour. It felt a bit light, but the engine, brakes, and suspension worked satisfactorily.

After the trip, I had a chance to talk to a new friend in Kuching. He said he had not heard of anyone who went below 170 kilometers per hour.

Tuan Haji came to see us off near the border of Bandar Seri Begawan. For the remaining distance, nobody took care of us. We organized the caravan ourselves and rode by ourselves. It was the tour company's job, but we didn't mind. We were always happy to spend time together.

Brunei and Malaysian immigration checkpoints in Sarawak were very efficient and much faster than the airport. We finally arrived at the hotel and it was already pitch black. We expected that the tour company would have prepared for us a great hotel complete with parking, but what we found was a budget hotel and roadside parking. Sigh...

For the program tonight, they wanted us to ride to the dinner venue after a shower. Nobody was pleased, so the tour company called Grab to pick us up. Only some went. The majority wanted to just take a walk to stretch their legs and relax after their all-day rides and just get something to eat near the hotel.

Day four of the journey - the distance was 245.1 kilometers. Because we were taken care of by people who understood the spirit of us riders and we also took care of each other, it was a great day. We were extremely happy about the trip.

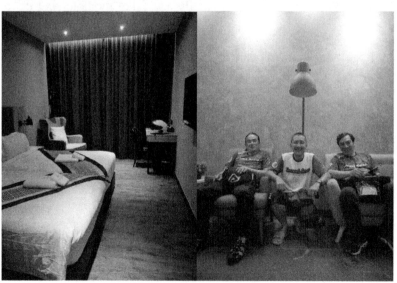

Chapter 14 Thailand's Reform May be the Wrong Solution

Day 5 of the trip. Today we traveled from Miri through Bintulu and would stay overnight in Sibu – the overall distance was 400 kilometers. Sarawak is home to the tour company. They have a lot of connections here. They know a lot of government officials and have started to flex their muscles since daybreak. We were to have breakfast with the Mayor of Miri. The restaurant that the tour company took us to didn't have a vegetarian menu, so I rode the yellow Ducati to eat at a Starbucks near the hotel.

When everyone had finished breakfast, it was time to prepare to depart. During that time, I saw a reporter waiting for an interview, so I approached to have a chat. The mayor also joined us in the conversation.

"I'm from Thailand. For motorcyclists, it's hard to find tourist information for this area, but a lot of people want to come. Even information for the ferry to Labuan or Brunei is hard to find on the internet. "

He continued to ask, "What do you think of our city?"

"I think that your city is very beautiful, and bigger than I thought. But I can't tell you more because I just arrived last night and this morning we already had to leave." I think it's a shame. A big, beautiful city -- We should have more time to explore Miri.

And it was time to leave. One by one, we started the engine. The badass yellow Ducati roared sweetly without complaint. The mayor marched to the beginning of the procession carrying the Sarawak flag. When everyone was ready, he waved the yellow, black, red, and white flags. The motorcycle's procession moved past the flag leaving the hotel gracefully.

The tour company continued to show their prowess of state connections. Immediately after entering the main road, police pickup trucks and large police motorcycles came to escort our convoy. At all intersections, everyone had to stop for us. The siren wailed loudly in the streets. Thundering throughout the city, we raced out of Miri at high speed. The siren drowned out all the sweet, powerful and badass roars. At over a hundred-kilometers-per-hour speed in the heart of the city, we leapt passed all intersections regardless of the lights. Everyone had to stop for us.

Hands on full throttle and full brakes, the vista of Miri, was replaced by the tail lights of the motorcycle ahead of me ... a 1,200cc, shaft-drive, Yamaha Super Ténéré, straddled by a skinny man from Penang named Rahman.

The police completed their mission at the edge of the city. We continued on with our own formation. Despite an effort to organize it, we didn't have the correct formation -- no marshal, no lead bike, no sweeper or tail bike, nor service vehicle - nothing. There was only a van that the tour company had rented to tail behind us, driven by Bob.

For some reason, the Yamaha Super Ténéré gang loved to ride at a very high speed, both Man (fictitious name), a big man from Phatthalung, and Rahman. Both were owners of red Super Ténérés. Not only that they loved to ride super-fast, but they seemed to think that others would also whisk through the wind as easily as they did.

But this is a Ducati Scrambler with no windshield, no suspension system with a perfectly set spring-sag. It has its own legend, its own history, but none of them involved the Paris-Dakar[11] ,like the Yamaha Super Ténérés.

The history of the Ducati Scrambler was about cool looks and relaxing street rides where there is electricity and civilization with beautiful girls turning their heads. It's not the history out in the boondock with dust and mud stains in the middle of nowhere like Paris-Dakar.

Phooey!

Finally, the yellow Ducati fell back to the end of the pack together with the massive golden-brown Harley-Davidson Backer with double square headlights aka shark face, ridden by a man wearing a Simpson's helmet. Both the bike and the helmet were all American culture. His name was Sabideen, a Muslim Sarawakian who loves freedom in a truly American fashion.

When Rahman decided to go at lightning speed, he was riding in front of the pack. Our feelings were like when our wives stopped nagging, happiness suddenly blossomed on our two-wheelers -- American and Italian.

This made me realize that perhaps the reason why Thai people are so unhappy, that the military has to return our happiness, may not be because of Thaksin, but our own wives.

But that's it -- when you think about too many things, you would need a reform - for Thailand, for Man, for Rahman, and for the wives – everything all tangled up. But there is still one good thing, one excellent thing.

So perfect that there is no need for reform ...

God damn me!

Chapter 15 American and Italian Kangaroos

We stopped for lunch at Bintulu. A few decades ago, Bintulu was a small, sleepy fishing town, but today it is a bustling trading center for natural gas with the busiest harbor in Sarawak. Incidentally, the tumult of Bintulu has increased -- not at the pier but on our dining table.

According to today's lunch program, the tour company arranged for us to have our meal while listening to a talk. The location and content were written ambiguously -- it wasn't clear if the talk was to promote the town or a sales pitch. But definitely it was not about tourist spots.

Steve, a well-built guy, owner of the three-inline-cylinder 800cc Triumph Tiger, decided not to attend the talk, but eat at a restaurant owned by a Bintulu-ian who loves to ride a motorcycle just like us. And after eating, Steve intended to leave immediately.

The tour company sat down to talk to Steve and the rest of the group. They tried to explain that arrangements had already been made. We could stop by a bit after lunch. Steve made it clear that everyone was free. Whoever wished to go on the tour program or go with Steve, could do so. Finally, we all agreed that we wanted to leave right away. We had our own reasons that the tour companies did not understand.

We arrived at Bintulu - which was half way at approximately 200 kilometers. We came by a small frontage road that ran along the seashore parallel to the Pan Borneo Highway AH150 that was under construction. Simply speaking, we had a beautiful small road bypassing the messy construction on the Pan Borneo Highway. But this afternoon, we could not avoid it and had to ride on the Pan Borneo Highway.

The remaining distance was 200 kilometers. Google Maps estimated four hours of travel time. If it rained, it would take longer. And the tour operator still wanted us to go and listen to the talk which was expected to finish at 2 p.m. Nobody wanted to ride on the road under messy construction, in a foreign place, in the rain with no service car following us at night. Even if we believed that the food was good, and the music sweet, we were not going.

Eventually, the tour operator grouchily stormed off from the table and left in the van with Bob. From Bintulu to Sibu, we had to travel on our own like in the morning. Only now there was no van running behind us. But we still had some luck. Sabideen, the owner of the American motorcycle and helmet, is a Sarawakian, born and raised in Borneo. He's a local biker.

So, this afternoon, he led us to bypass the Pan Borneo Highway that was under construction via a small road that was not on Google Map's suggestions. The small road was called Jin Kuala Tatau, and it runs through the village and along the beach, helping us avoid the Pan Borneo Highway for quite a while, but not all of it. We also had an additional 40 kilometers of detour.

This road is indeed quite special and extraordinary. It cuts through the water and probably because the road was near the sea, it was inundated with water. The waterway was built with a large pipe under the road. And for some reason, the connecting points between the road and the pipe were uneven just like that gap between the commoners and the aristocrats[12].

The common folk who have constantly been fighting against the economy and were only getting poorer, lower, are ordinary roads. The upper class are like the road above the pipeline that does not feel any economic impact whatsoever causing inequality between the classes. Much like the political problems in Thailand, this has caused severely uneven pavement all over town just like on Jin Kuala Tatau Road, Malaysia.

The Ducati Scrambler followed behind the local biker, the golden-brown Harley-Davidson. I was in the second position of the procession. And all of a sudden, the 400 kg. minus its rider Harley-Davidson, bounced up in the air.

Oy...??!! 'What kind of Harley jumps like a kangaroo?'

My eyelids rapidly shot open, my heart was pounding, and my blood was pumping. Fear was dominating my brain while it was trying to come up with some plausible explanations. The word it came up with best summed up the situation,

'Holy Shit!'

The front wheel that was inflated at thirty-three PSI banged into something. My hands holding super tight on the handlebars, my feet on the foot pegs, I pushed myself to stand up. Then the Scrambler, half the weight of a giant Harley, leapt up into the air, like an Italian kangaroo following hot on the heels of the American kangaroo.

Um ...I survived it. But before I could think further, the American kangaroo then jumped up again. I clutched my handlebars tightly commanding the two four-cylinder Brembo brakes to engage right away. Not an instant sooner, the front wheel touched the bridge. I quickly released the brakes, pushing myself to stand up.

The brain still produced the same words, 'Holy Shit!'

My heart was still fully pumping blood. Fear still firmly gripped me and the badass yellow Ducati was jumping like a kangaroo again. After four, five times of American and Italian kangaroo jumps, my brain started to produce different words.

'Ha Ha Ha. Kangaroo motorcycle. So much fun!'

The rhythm of my heart started to relax. My mood changed from fear to excitement, from disaster to fun.

The Harley Kangaroo began to slow down. The Ducati kangaroo also reduced speed. But the inline-three-cylinders, eight-hundred-cc Triumph Tiger of Dr. Herman's did not need to do that. With its impeccable suspension, the Triumph Tiger did not have to jump like a kangaroo, but slither through the violent bump just like its namesake.

Dr. Herman still fed the three-cylinder to spit out fierce sound and horsepower ceaselessly while overtaking the Ducati kangaroo. While waiting to overtake the Harley kangaroo, another gigantic bridge appeared and an eighteen-wheeler was in the oncoming traffic. And we just overtook another eighteen-wheeler a few seconds ago. It was right behind us on a narrow two-lane road…nowhere to pull over.

The three-cylinder tiger outmaneuvered the bridge with some reaction but no problem. But there was one thing, however, that decided not to continue on with Dr. Herman.

<u>Chapter 16 The American Kangaroo's Side Pouch</u>

It was Dr. Herman's rain jacket that flew out from under the seat, tumbling over in the middle of the road.

The day before, on the way back from the Tip of Borneo, I noticed a license plate in the middle of the road, but didn't think it concerned us. But when we got back to the hotel, it turned out that the license plate of Palan's, the owner of the classic Triumph Bonneville, had gone missing.

I saw that and laughed while telling him, "I think I saw a license plate on the road, but didn't think it belonged to any of us."

"You should have told me," he said.

The situation right in front of me was exactly as I had described. One eighteen-wheeler was oncoming, and we just overtook another eighteen-wheeler that was now behind us. The road was narrow with enough room for cars in both directions with no shoulders to park.

Thirty-six large wheels, spinning fast on a small road. Instinctively, stopping to retrieve one's belongings wasn't a good idea. So, we kept on following the Harley kangaroo.

A while after that, Dr. Herman dashed forward to overtake the Harley and then other motorcycles followed suit with their on-point suspension system.

Rahman's Yamaha Super Ténéré also passed by comfortably without him having to stand up.

The BMW K-1600 owned by Philip, a Malaysian, also passed easily at high speed.

The small BMW Adventure and Vincent's GS800 also sped through in a smooth, elegant, manner.

There was nothing to be said about the Kings of Adventures that are widely known to have the best suspension system in the world -- the air-cooled BMW GS1150 belonging to Fu and Resuan. They breezed through the brutal bumps just like the Frog Citroën with hydraulic suspension well-deserving of their world-class reputation.

Tum came with his wife Helen. Both were Chinese Malaysian riding a 750cc Honda -- the latest model in the market. It's the world's first redefined motorcycle that combines a scooter, a big bike and an adventure bike into a shape somewhat like it's ready to transform into a robot named XADV. Tum owns many motorcycles, one of which is BMW GS with Boxer engine. When asked to compare the suspension systems, he said that the Honda XADV has an impressive suspension second only to his BMW GS.

The Kawasaki of Calvin- a British guy who came with his lovely Indonesian Muslim wife, had left since morning. We had no idea how they were doing.

There were only the American Becker, the Italian Scrambler, and the Aristocratic British Bonneville who had to negotiate the merciless bumps in fun kangaroo hops.

Not long after, Sabideen's Harley-Davidson started to act up. While in a free fall back onto the pavement after jumping over one of the rough bridge entrances, his left bag opened. All his belongings flew out and littered the road. Horns were blaring for the procession to stop. Those who overtook us doubled back. We helped each other pick up all the things on the road with a lot of laughter.

We rode on for a while and then stopped for refreshments at a small town called Balingian on the bank of a slow-flowing big river reminiscing of the Ping River in my hometown. This city is Sabideen's birthplace and he decided to end the trip here not because it was his home but because of the tour company.

Sabideen is a member of the Borneo Harley-Davidson Motorcycle Club. It overlapped with the Harley-Davidson Labuan Motorcycle Club -- the one that told the tour company to take a hike and go back to the hotel on the day we got to Labuan. That event very much displeased the tour company and they took it out on Sabideen. The tour company said that they didn't want Sabideen to be part of the caravan anymore, but Steve, who was quite Americanized (having lived in the U.S. for some time) intervened and prevented the tour company from treating Sabideen that way.

Two days had passed and the tour company still continued to give Sabideen the stink eye. He didn't need to endure such uncivilized treatment and decided to end the trip in his hometown. We said goodbye and lovingly promised that should we find ourselves in each other's hometown, we would be greeted with the utmost hospitality

We continued on our journey with about 160 kilometers remaining and we needed to head back onto the Pan Borneo Highway. The ones left were those who love to live freely with the wind, sunshine and motorcycles. We didn't have any problems and were happy to spend time together.

As soon as we entered the Pan Borneo Highway, it was clear why the locals had advised us to avoid many bridge constructions. All the bypasses were dirt roads -- and there were a lot of them. The roads that weren't bypasses were full of potholes. Trucks run back and forth to haul dirt and construction materials. All the graders, tractors, water trucks, were working diligently.

The time was now around four o'clock. Even in the afternoon with bright sunlight, the bypasses were hard to spot. So, it would be out of question at night, and should be avoided at all cost. And the tour company did not understand this at all. The Ducati was speeding, breaking, dodging, all the while never going beyond the fourth gear, full of caution. After a while, it got used to the situation and started to be mischievous.

Once the naughtiness started, craziness ensued.

Chapter 17 The Sensual Hip-Shaking of the Ducati in Heat

We rode behind a BMW GS1150 belonging to the ad hoc marshal, named Resuan. He had attended many training courses on motorcycle riding with BMW. One of them was riding in the marshal position or as a lead rider of the procession. He rode smoothly and confidently, so I followed him with a peace of mind.

The Ducati was under the highest traction control to maneuver through the countless and messy bypasses both on and off road. I could twist the accelerator in any manner, the electronic control system would keep the front and rear wheels in sync. A flashing amber light on the dashboard indicated that the control was at work. So, I could follow the BMW with sufficient confidence. Often, I intentionally accelerated to engage the function. It's a must have and once you have it, you have to use it.

Robert Kiyosaki, the author of the *Rich Dad, Poor Dad*, once wrote: *The opposite of risk is control.* But too much control is no fun. With increased confidence, I turned down the traction control to one level lower. The system would allow the wheels to spin out of synch a little but not too much, and they were still under the system's control.

Upon leaving the dirt bypass to enter the paved road, there would be some loose gravel on the surface making it quite skiddy. As soon as I accelerated, the Ducati was responding to please her master by transferring some horsepower to the Pirelli tires, causing a tailspin. This gave her master such fun. Then the electronic control would try to cut the engine to correct the course preventing her from shaking her hips even further.

The Ducati's sound at second and third gear started from a low rumble of low RPMs. The two-cylinder L-twin engine and no-spring antique valve groaned over the badass, melodious sound from her twin exhaust pipes -- music to my ear ...tack, tack, tack, tack.

The combination of stress over making time before dark and the lack of off-road experience coupled with monitored risk, the tail spins and the engine groans of strong effort to leap forward through the exhaust pipes was the most enjoyable. I smiled under the helmet. Simply speaking, this was stressful fun.

After a while of drudging through the dirt road, Steve's Triumph Tiger was overtaking to the lead position while sending a hand signal to notify Resuan, who was leading the caravan to stop. We parked along the road that was under construction away from traffic. Since there were a lot of us, we needed to find enough space for all of us to park.

Steve's motorcycle had a little problem and required tools to fix. Beside the tools that came with each bike, nobody prepared more than that because they understood from the tour program that a service car would accompany us. Coincidentally, the yellow Ducati had more tools than others as she came from farther away. So, we took care of the situation, but this made us ponder the question that should the problems be more serious, what would we do?

And then we continued on. But, Resuan, the ad hoc marshal, was not ready to start.

"I'll just go ahead, okay? Just overtake me." The yellow Ducati and her master then went on to squiggle in front, having fun, confidence boosted.

With increased confidence, came higher speed. Looking at the rearview mirror, I saw a couple of bikes behind me. There was no sign of Resuan. The sun was about to set. I decided not to wait and kept on spinning about like a horny animal having fun with full confidence.

Resuan was still nowhere to be found, but my confidence was magnified. When confidence magnified, so did the speed. And with intensified speed, came the highway patrol. Two Hondas with gigantic fairings and four-cylinder-inline engines were parked there, blue sirens flashing. Standing on the right, they waved us in. I thought to myself that if the couple of bikes that followed me didn't stop, I wouldn't stop either. Having thought so, I twisted the accelerator some more while buckling along pretending to be oblivious to the HPs.

Passing by the HPs, I glanced at the rearview mirror. The bikes following me didn't stop. So, I kept darting forward until I reached the junction to turn into the city. If Resuan still wasn't here, I'd stop and wait for the rest of them here. I got to the intersection leading to the city and stopped at the traffic light. Then I turned right. Resuan was still not there. I put on the left turn signal to park on the shoulder and turned to look back at the intersection. My heart sank. The HPs' motorcycles were coming toward me, sirens blaring. My friends were all riding behind them. I understood right away. They had come to escort me to town.

Rahman, the owner of the blue Super Ténéré, waved to me to join them and get back into the procession. And all of us were under the power of the tour company again. The motorcycle convoy sped into Sibu city at high speed. Every traffic light, every intersection, every roundabout, the whole city had to stop for us as the ear-splitting siren drowned out the exhaust of every brand. The Siren, the big kahuna.

At the hotel, I asked to take a photo with the highway patrols before checking into the four-star hotel next to the big river called Rajang. This majestic river reminded me of the Chao Phraya River in Bangkok. I took a shower, then leaned back to rest while contemplating Sibu, a large city by the river -- beautiful or not? Who knows?

Throughout Sibu, I only spotted the two round tail lights of the Yamaha Ténéré.

Chapter 18 So Sorry I Cannot Follow the Path that Others Love

According to our program, dinner this evening was going to be at the hotel's rooftop restaurant overlooking the river. The al fresco ambiance should be beautiful with the river as a backdrop. I walked in at 8pm as scheduled and found some of the guys browsing the menu looking extremely upset. "If they prepared the food like this, I'd rather find something to eat myself," he said. After a while, the rest of us arrived. After I had looked at the menu, I decided I should go out to find something to eat by myself as well, but because I was curious to learn about the next day's program, I decided to attend the meeting first before going out. I was wrong.

Steve and Dr. Herman were giving the tour company hell, lambasting them without hesitation, in both English and Chinese, for failing to provide service vehicles earlier that day. This created tremendous uneasiness for everyone and marred the atmosphere of the meeting. I proposed a change of approach by meeting among ourselves first to list what it was that we wanted and then meet with the tour company afterwards to avoid disagreement and maintain a good atmosphere for dinner.

But Steve and Dr. Herman viewed the service vehicle, the correct formation, and all the other arrangements as announced by the tour company as matters that concern our safety and are therefore of utmost importance. Hence, they needed to be discussed instantly -- which was true. Had there been a punctured tire or that we had run out of gas –all of which were possible- it would have become a very big deal.

The tour company was offended by the harsh criticism they received to the point that they were willing to end the tour right then and there. Intense arguments went on for the next two hours without any conclusion. I was famished and fatigued so I went out to find something to eat near the hotel and went straight to bed. Today was the fifth day of our journey -- we rode from Miri to Sibu for a total of 440 kilometers.

Morning came, the hotel breakfast was much better than the meal we had last night putting everyone in a much happier mood. At the time of departure, the program was still unclear. The atmosphere continued to simmer from the night before. The state authorities gathered in front of the hotel waiting to wave the flag to release the procession. The highway patrol car was already idling around ready to take us out of town at high speed.

Some of us were standing next to our bikes, some were straddling them, but had not started the engine. Some already started the engine, ready to leave, but then switched it off again. The tour company had laid out a route for us to travel on the Pan Borneo Highway, stop for lunch with the state authorities, and local politicians before continuing on to Kuching.

From the research I did last night, we had two routes to choose from: the first route was the one that the tour company had prepared for us, via the Pan Borneo Highway. The second route, Google Map suggested that we ride through Maludam National Park and take a ferry twice.

No matter how many times I looked, Google insisted that we take the second route. It seemed that if Google could speak, it would probably curse the person who thought of taking the first route. I could not answer myself which one was a better route, because the second route needed us to take the ferry twice -- and details could not be found online. But from looking at the map, the second route is definitely more charming than the first.

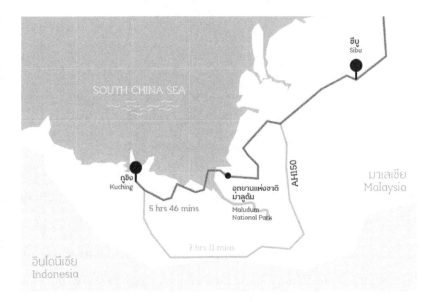

I had to talk to someone.

Steve had his own route this morning, but his was neither the first, nor the second. He wanted to take his bike to check the tires, brakes, chains, oil levels and bolts. Steve's bike had a problem yesterday. He wanted to make sure that his Tiger was ready to leap forward.

The situation in front of the hotel became increasingly tense. The state authority was hanging on to the flag and the highway patrol were ready to turn on the sirens. I felt we had to leave. No matter which route we would choose, we had to leave. So, I proposed that we leave here and follow Steve to the motorcycle garage, and then carry on our discussion there. Everybody agreed, so we started our engines.

When the procession was ready, the governor waved the flag, the sirens started shrieking, and everyone was slowly riding out of the hotel. A firm order from the lead patrol car commanded all vehicles on the road to stop. The lead car dashed out. The garage was within a walking distance from the hotel, so Steve didn't follow. He rode slowly, and put on his left-turn signal and parked at a motorcycle repair shop on the street behind the hotel and all the bikes followed. The lead patrol car stopped in the middle of the road, and turned to look and understood that we wanted to check our bikes a little before the trip.

Some of the guys checked their motorcycles themselves, but Steve's was being closely examined. I'm confident in the yellow Ducati. I had been preparing at my best in Chiang Mai -- new tires, new sprocket chain, new engine oil, and I asked my mechanics to anticipate that there would be no trouble in the next 10,000 kilometers.

For this trip, I only rode about 2,000 kilometers. Maintenance of the Ducati was not what I looked for. I needed route information and ferry information. If you ask ordinary car drivers, they'd answer like car drivers. We ride motorcycles, and do not want the roads that are suitable for cars. We need the roads befitting of our motorcycles. So, I saw two people on two motorcycles -- the highway patrols who were escorting us out of town.

"You love riding motorcycles, I also love riding motorcycles. I have some questions about the route. Can I ask you about it?" The highway patrols didn't speak much English, but one of our guys came to help translate, "I checked on Google and there are two routes. Which one do you think people who love to ride motorcycles would be happier?"

The police responded clearly, and simply translated as, "For the second route the small road is better." He continued, "The Pan Borneo Highway is under construction. you won't have fun."

"What about the ferry? Does it run all the time? We have to take the ferry twice."

"Yes. The ferries run all day. No worries."

My face was now beaming with a smile, so were the patrols.

Everyone seemed more relaxed after having had their bikes checked. We took a group picture with the Huawei Tom Yum camera with cheerful smiles on our face.

was clear and had all the answers to prepare to talk to the tour company and my friends. I was thinking of a song by Thai pop superstar, Toon Bodyslam.

"So sorry I cannot follow the path that others love. Today, I won't walk on your path, but I'm all for the one I chose today."

It was fine for people to choose their own paths, but I was fully committed to the second route -- finding my own food, filling my own gas, taking the ferry myself. Today, I didn't follow the tour's path that they thought was good, and I was all for my chosen path.

Chapter 19 An Offer that Cannot be Refused

I realized that it already was late and wanted to leave, so I told my friends, "We have two options, the first route, the Pan Borneo Highway, over 400 kilometers, and the duration of which is about an hour and a half longer than the second, according to Google. The second route is a small road through the national park. The distance is about 300 kilometers. I am not a local, and don't know what the road will be like, and if there will be any problems crossing by the ferries. But I inquired with the two highway patrols who love motorcycling just like us and they suggested the second route. I will take the second route. Whoever wants to take the first route, the patrols and the tour company are waiting. Let's leave right now. We're already late."

No one walked over to start the engine. Nobody opted to go on the first route.

The tour company told me that "I never knew there were two routes. You are very good. If I organize another program, please consider being our consultant."

I replied, "Let's see about this time first." But deep inside I thought, 'The hell I will.'

And the tour operator said, "Okay, let's take the second route. I'll go and talk to the patrols. They will lead us to it. As for our luncheon appointment, I will take care of it. "

Then we left the beautiful city of Sibu (maybe). The sirens were echoing throughout the city again. People stopped for us at every intersection, every traffic light, every roundabout just like before. The only change was that BMW GS 1150's tail lights that belonged to the ad hoc marshal, Resuan took place of the Ténéré's tail lights.

A little while after we left town, the highway patrolmen made a U-turn. Our route was a beautiful small road. The traffic was light and it was relaxing. The road was very pleasing to bikers exactly like the two highway patrolmen told us. It was not long before we arrived at the ferry pier that would take us across the estuary into the Maludam National Park.

The ferry had no schedule, but it ran back and forth connecting the route all day long. Just after a short wait, we were on board. And not even the yellow Ducati's engine had cooled down, we already docked at the national park. Over ten motorcycles gradually left the ferry and headed straight to the park.

We were going to ride through this national park to board a ferry on the other side to Kuching. The park is on the edge of the sea. Looking at the map, we would see it as a headland. But even though we were riding almost at the edge of the sea, we couldn't see it, because of the lush greenery of the banana trees and coconut trees densely grown alongside the road. The deep blue sky was bright and cheerful just like all beach skies. The beautiful road, paved in black, was smooth, but not even. The surface was adulated because of the condition of the muddy soil near the sea. Our bikes didn't have any problem. They just bobbed up and down gleefully. It was a great ride. The van was experiencing some trouble. It turned into a kangaroo van. The people in the van kept becoming weightless, and jerked around.

It was not long before we arrived at the second ferry terminal. Getting off the ferry, we stopped for lunch at a small shoreline town called Sebuyau, just over a hundred kilometers from the hotel in Kuching, our destination for today. We've already covered over half of the way.

The lunch was good. The lemon tea was refreshing and tasted great. Everyone was satisfied with the road that we were just on. But the happiness was short-lived and we had an argument with the tour company again. Apart from the fact that the tour company couldn't understand simple things, it still was excellent at creating problems. They changed the hotel in Kuching. We kind of had it with the hotel change in Miri. It was not the hotel in the program, but changed to reduce the budget. And that left us with horrendous parking. Even though the hotel was confident that our bikes would not be lost, all the fixtures on the bikes are extremely expensive and could very easily get stolen. The tour company and the hotel did not understand this.

The new hotel was about 30 kilometers outside the city, so we asked them to change back to the original place. The tour company said they would check. After checking, they said that the car park was full. Some of us didn't believe it. So, they called to talk to the hotel and the hotel confirmed that there was proper parking space indeed. Finally, we decided to stay at the same hotel as specified in the tour package.

Full, but not satisfied, we continued our journey. Before leaving, we needed to stop for gas. The tour company had to fill us up, and when we reached a small, classic-looking Shell station, we lined up to have our tanks filled. The attendant seemed to be wearing both petrol pump boy's and the owner's hats. He was shirtless and enjoying the fact that a lot of unique motorcycles lined up at his pump. I marveled at classic old signs.

The small town with a blend of vintage looks and western cowboy mood with the Shell logo. When it was time to pay, the tour company had already disappeared. So, we had to pay for it ourselves.

Then we finally reached the last leg of entering Kuching. The small road took us through a number of small villages. When there were no villages, the road was flanked by palm trees, bananas and coconut trees. The road was smooth, with no big bumps or brutal bridges. We rode with so much fun at about a hundred kilometers per hour. As we approached the city, the state authority that the tour operator had at their beck and call was waiting for us.

My patience ran out. I didn't want to go into town at high speed and see Kuching through the tail lights of my friend's motorcycle. I sped the badass, yellow Ducati up next to Resuan and signaled to stop for refreshments. I intended to park and talked to the patrolmen to bring us into town like other ordinary citizens and stop at traffic lights just like everyone else so that we could appreciate the nature of the streets and traffic in Kuching like ordinary people. The ad hoc marshal didn't stop. He sent a signal back that the police were leading us, we couldn't stop.

No matter what, I would not enter the cat city of Kuching this way. I made a firm decision, decelerating the yellow Ducati to keep on the left. I waved for everyone to pass me until the last one. There was a patrol vehicle at the back. I turned on the left turn signal light, then slowed down and stepped on the brake so that the brake lights lit up, removed my right hand from the accelerator and waved for the patrols to pass.

When the patrol was next to me, I applied my right hand on the brakes, commanded the Brembo with eight pistons on the front wheel and one on the rear wheel to work hard immediately. The Ducati's speed dropped dramatically because of the Brembo brakes' excellent performance. It worked exactly as the engineers designed it and not allowing the police to exercise the state power to order me back into the procession.

The police looked in his rearview mirror. I waved, insisting that they kept on going. State authority has to go with the majority. I was just a minority, so the police had to leave me behind. Making an offer he could not refuse was successful. The yellow Ducati and her master, dropped out of the aristocratic class to be a lowly commoner, heading into the cat city of Kuching just like ordinary people would.

Chapter 20 Art Engineering & Curve Engineering

I dropped the speed to about 80 kilometers per hour. Hot air pushed against my face. To my left and right were abundant, verdant tropical forests -- as rumored. Not long after that, the road expanded to four large lanes. The badass yellow Ducati purred her charming sound, seeming happy and content with how things were going. We passed through many universities, schools, and neighborhood's shophouse projects similar to my family business in Chiang Mai. I decided to stop for some cold refreshments and check out the projects -- maybe I could put this on my expense account as fact-finding trips in the same way as how it's being done in some countries.

Shophouses here, if they were new projects, I have not seen any of them built right on the street with street parking. Even with only twenty rooms facing the road, they are built with separate entrance and parking spaces. But if it's in the city or the old town, it's similar to our Gad Luang (Central Market in Chiang Mai).

A cold drink helped quench my thirst that was intensified by the heat. The parked yellow Ducati was there flaunting her body. Some teenage boys sitting in nearby shops turned to look and made comments -- a typical reaction of those who admired the two-wheeled soul crafts and had to look when some unique ones came into view. It must be like how an average Thai man can't help ogling at curvaceous girls whenever they appear in sight.

The Ducati's concave proportions, the Pirelli peg-patterned tires, the Brembo disc brakes and the chunky double pipes are beautiful and befitting of the reputation of the country that designed it. It is the perfect blending of art and engineering by top engineers. It'd call it art engineering. The engineers who are the owners of such masterpieces must be happy that their work is admired by people.

131

The same thing goes for the vital measurements of a famous Thai sex symbol like Aum-Patcharapa. She reveals some parts while concealing others, showing off her skin and curves. The curves and beautiful colors are truly attractive, seductive, and simply irresistible. It's a blend of curves and art by God -- a curve engineering that sparks lustful flames in your heart. God, the Master of such a fine piece of art must be happy that His work is so admired.

I had just had a cold drink, why was I feeling hot again?... I'd better journey on.

The yellow Ducati roared her bullying sound as I pressed the red Start button on the right handlebar. We were heading toward Kuching city. As we got closer, the traffic and the roadside houses started to get denser. We passed a large shopping mall with several familiar brand labels.

Many roundabouts had come into my life to give me more practice. Some were so gigantic that if we were to put the White Pagoda in front of the American Consulate in Chiang Mai at the center, the road shoulder would be all across the Ping river reaching the Mae Jaru's (fictitious name) house near Wat Si Khong. The traffic became heavier as we entered the city, but it wasn't as bad as Bangkok. It was more like Chiang Mai, my hometown.

We passed the majestic cat monument, showing off the Kuching's identity in the middle of the road. I then turned left into the hotel along the Sarawak River. It was a mighty river the size of the Chao Phraya River. Kuching was born and had grown up because of this river.

My eyes swept around to look for my friends' bikes but only found the BMW GS1150 that perhaps belonged to Resuan, parked there. I didn't see the rest. I rode the

Ducati up to take a closer look, uncertain if I had come to the right hotel, but I tried to check in any way.

Once I opened the door and entered the place I was sure it was the right hotel, because the Marketing Manager came over to greet me. Having been on the bikes for so many days, when I saw a beautifully made-up lady in a lovely dress coming over to greet and welcome me, I had to really try to control my behavior, my gaze and manners. Still, I couldn't help it and had to ask for a photo with her.

Before I could take the elevator up to my room, the police motorcycles blasting the ear-splitting sirens annoyingly led our group to turn into the hotel. Even I who was a member of the same group felt that it was such a nauseating display of power by the privileged and entitled. How would the residents of Miri, Sibu and Kuching feel?

While waiting for my friends to come in, I asked Resuan "Why didn't you go with them?

Resuan said, "I got left behind by the procession and couldn't catch up so I looked at the map and came to the hotel myself."

As my friends came in one by one, I asked if the patrolmen had taken them to sightsee around town. Maybe the tour company finally came around with their work. But I had too high hopes. They were late because the tour operator had not communicated with the lead patrol car, so they were taken to the original hotel.

Calvin, a British man who had been working at Petronas for over twenty years and came with his wife Lea, an Indonesian Muslim, told us that, "The patrol guys were having so much fun to be honest. I think the cops must be so bored at their desk jobs."

The hotel occupied a great location in the heart of the city, near the activity area, similar to our Tha Phae Gate activity area. My bedroom window overlooked the beautiful Sarawak River. A gorgeously designed suspension bridge stretched in the middle of the vast river. Its beauty was second to none both in the western or eastern world.

In fact, if any bridge lovers saw this, they would vote for this exquisitely designed suspension bridge to be more beautiful than Chompu (a famous movie star) for sure. But for me who had been riding for many days and didn't get to see enough lovely women, my vote went straight to Chompu as more beautiful without much thought.

On the other side stood a large and beautiful building. I checked the map but didn't quite get what it was. I later learned that it was a local parliament building, the central administrative quarter of the government -- grand, majestic, and awe-inspiring. It was the parliament building whose beauty was second to none in the world -- a landscape that truly adds elegance to the city. ...

Steve sent a message to our WhatsApp group saying that he was going to eat at a restaurant within walking distance from the hotel and tagged me adding "there is vegetarian food too."

I took a shower, lay down a bit and talked to Nusara, then went down to the lobby. I found a couple of friends there, so we walked together. There was some nice street art in front of the restaurant to photograph.

But when I opened the door, I got goosebumps and cried out loud, not caring about anyone,

"Oh, By George ..."

Chapter 21 More than Good Food and Great Music that can be had without Closing the Airport

A Life-size Formula One was hung on the wall of the restaurant. A real, beautiful, and classy sapphire-color Ferrari, the first Honda Africa Twin built to conquer the Paris-Dakar race, the two-stroke Honda NSR -- the motorcycle that is still in the hearts of many people around the world, BMW with Boxer HP2 engine, Moto Guzzi cafe racer, Two Moto Guzzi Cafe Racer, Bimota DB7, Vespa Side Cars, real helmets were on display everywhere along with many races trophies, and posters about motorcycle speed, cars, racing cars, boats and adventurous travel.

The space between each automotive engineering was no slouch. Each was a dining table. Light beams shone on each of them displaying their power, designs, their mission of speed, exquisitely and tastefully. This was not a restaurant where cars are parked, but a magnificent car park with a restaurant in it. If Chompu and Aum (two of Thailand's best-known sexy movie stars) were to sit and dine in this restaurant, their beauty would be eclipsed by the aura from these engineering marvels.

All my friends were sitting at the dining table with a couple of unfamiliar faces. I was so thrilled that I couldn't stop walking around, could not stop admiring those engineering marvels. Finally, Steve must have seen that this country bumpkin was just too wide-eyed about all the flamboyance, that he couldn't see the person sitting at the head of the table, the restaurant owner himself!

Steve dragged me to be introduced to the restaurateur. Just from looking at the restaurant and those automotive jewels, it was clear that he was not just a regular guy but a character straight out of Gu Long's novels -- maybe not Lu Xiaofeng because he had no affiliation, but he must be somebody of the same caliber as the Master of White Cloud Castle, or the dignified and enigmatic gentleman in white robe, Ximen Chuixue.

His name was 'Alex Wong'. Even though I wanted to talk to him, I couldn't take my eyes off the gleaming bright lights of these automobiles. Alex Wong must have seen this obsession. In fact, he must have had the same obsession just like the old adage, 'Takes one to know one'. Alex Wong took me for a tour of the restaurant and introduced me to each of the extraordinary engineering wonders.

"All the vehicles are in perfect condition and still running. This one, I don't let it run even though it works well. I intend to add it to my collection. This is a special edition BMW with HP 2 Boxer engine -- really powerful, and sounds very sweet. It's one of those I ride regularly."

We started to get to know each other, he asked me "Where in Thailand are you from?"

"I live in Chiang Mai. Do you know Chiang Mai? "

"Of course. A couple of months ago, I just drove the 911[13] to travel around. stayed at the Dusit Hotel near the Night Bazaar. I toured the north, and spent more than ten days in Chiang Mai. One day, I rode on highway 1148[14]. The scenery was so breathtaking. Even after riding the whole stretch, I still didn't have enough and turned around to do it all over again. I posted my photos on Facebook too."

"I'm not on Facebook, but my wife is. What's your Facebook name? I'd like to add you as a friend."

Facebook allows one account to have a maximum of five thousand friends. Alex Wong had three remaining. He accepted Nusara as his friend. These days, he still likes her posts. He is currently on a BMW motorcycle adventure trip in Europe.

The restaurant was excellent. Vegetarian food was not a problem. The choice of music being played was lovely. -- the food was good, the music was great, the automobiles were amazing, the atmosphere was good without any kind of airport closures[15] involved!

After the meal, a few friends and I went for a walk along the riverbank, checking out the light and sound show with the dancing fountain. We saw the BMW group at a nice little restaurant. While we came with a fake tour company, the BMW Group came with a professional one. This was their first day. Those who love motorcycling just like us flew from all over the world and they just had a briefing -- a professional one. Everyone was happy, the food was excellent. They were waiting to see the signature show of Kuching, just as scheduled by the BMW tour program.

Silas took me around the dining room and introduced me to many of the motorcycle lovers and then invited me to take part in an auspicious ceremony of Sarawak. The ceremony involved drinking wine. I normally don't drink alcohol during my trips, but this was a fun and sacred ceremony with those whose souls are driven by motorcycles.

God will understand. God always understands. This is a ritual of the motorcycle religion in Sarawak.

After shouting some gibberish three times, we downed the wine in shot glasses and the holy ceremony ended with a lot of fun and I made one more friend. I had a good feeling about Silas and only knew later that apart from being in charge of this BMW tour, he was also a training coach at BMW.

This was the first day of our trip that we arrived back at the hotel at a decent hour. So, we had time to stroll around to experience the city's highlights in the evening. It was the first day that we had a happy evening, watching the spectacular fountain show, chatting with foreign friends who love living on two wheels in a beautiful city.

Day six of the journey - the distance covered today was 318.7 kilometers. From tomorrow onward, we'd travel to Indonesia and back to finish our trip in this city. After the tour is over, I might have a night or two to travel with Nusara a bit before taking the Ducati to board the ferry at Kuching to return to Port Klang.

When I got back to the hotel, I called Nusara. This city is very beautiful with good hotels, good food, good music, good automobiles, good shows, and the airport is not closed.

Nusara started to wane from her "go far away" mood. She was planning a trip to Kuching because she missed me. Aha!! Before dropping off to sleep that night, I told Nusara in my heart, "Come close to me," and slept tight that night dreaming about Chompu (the sexy movie star).

Chapter 22 Can We Cross Over to Indonesia? ... I Don't Know.

This morning was the seventh day of our journey. As scheduled, we woul depart for Indonesia from the city of Kuching, the state of Sarawak, Malaysia, vi Sambas and stay overnight in Singkawang. The approximate distance was 27 kilometers which Google estimated should take us five hours.

Crossing over to Indonesia was clearly stated in the tour program. For severa days, Steve and Dr. Herman had been asking the tour company for our custom documents. The Brunei local head honcho like Tuan Haji and even the Sarawakian bi; cheese, Sabideen knew that crossing over to Indonesia would require a custom document or CPD (*Carnet de Passages en Douane*)[16] -- without it, you would not b able to cross. From what I gathered from their website, CPD is quite difficult to obtain You must make a security deposit which could be as much as three times the value o the vehicles. It is the consensus among many countries that a CPD is required in orde to bring personal vehicles across the border. In some countries, this is not requirement, but it is clear that for Indonesia, it is a must.

The tour company simply told us to wait and see. But from our experience we didn't have much confidence that they would be successful. It could not be denie that they had a great relationship with government agencies and could convenientl leverage that relationship. At each of the cities that we passed through, all the police highway patrols, and governors gave us excellent facilitation. The brochure also showed Sarawak Tourism Board's logo, and the tour company's Facebook posts also showed pictures of their agents with different government officials.

But the tour company did not give us any further reassurance. The previou night, they announced among the group that they would not go to Indonesia with u;

and gave us the phone number for the guide who would meet and take care of us after our successful crossing into Indonesia. When we asked for a reason, the tour operator simply replied, "Kuching is my home, and I have been traveling for several days now. I miss my home and want to go to sleep in my own bed. But don't worry. I already sent plane tickets to Tuan Haji and Sabideen to fly to Kuching. Both of them will take the van to Indonesia with you."

Today was our departure day. Tension pervaded the air. We had breakfast at the hotel. Clearly, there was a split of opinions into two: one was "Not going" because they were certain that we could not cross; and the other, "Going" according to the program. If we could not cross, we would waste one day and the tour company must be responsible.

The tour company invited us all to our motorcycles. We saw two people with them. From the way they dressed, we could guess these guys were from some state agencies. And the tour company started briefing, "This is the Consul General of Indonesia. His consulate is in Kuching, Sarawak and this is the assistant consul. They will advise us on traveling to Indonesia today "

The Consul General said his greetings, and the assistant consul began to explain. "We had submitted a case that you all are our guests. We are the Indonesian consulate here. Therefore, all of you are entering Indonesia under our responsibility."

"Normally, bringing a car or a motorcycle from another country to drive in Indonesia requires a CPD." he continued.

"No, CPD, No Go," the assistant consul explained clearly, matching Steve's research.

Then, he went on softly, "It is not a hundred percent that you will get into the country. It all depends on the discretion of the customs officer at the checkpoint. But our confidence level is high. We do not anticipate any problems."

The Consul General nodded and made eye contact to reaffirm the assistant consul statements. Our level of confidence increased a great deal, and so did that of the first group who thought of not going. Steve smiled. But he was still concerned, because we also needed another document. This document would not be used in

Indonesia, but needed on the Malaysian side. The tour company could not produce it, but merely told us not to worry.

Steve and the rest of us told the tour operator to travel with us. He said okay, and the mood became more relaxed and friendlier. We took a group picture with the Indonesian Consul General and the assistant consul, then went to our motorcycles. Bob, the van driver came over dutifully. The Ducati needed some mascara to be applied to her chain. To shed weight, Ducati engineers did away with double kickstands. Her side stand arched beautifully. It had a sleek design, but very delicate. Using the side stand to raise the rear wheel could bend or damage it, so I just pushed her forward slowly. Bob followed along to spray the chain lubricant.

With just one push of the start button, her engine roared the badass rumble to dare the trans-border route. She clearly expressed her wish to go to Indonesia.

We formed a procession. When everyone was ready, the Ambassador waved the flag, and so, the journey began. We headed out of Kuching straight to the Indonesian border, via the Pan Borneo Highway under construction -- a duel between tiny human beings and the inexplicable, almighty God.

Once we reached the exit from the Pan Borneo Highway to the checkpoint, the van disappeared from the procession. We thought the driver couldn't keep up, but he was a local and would probably catch up eventually. So, when all the motorcycles were present, we took the exit on the left from the Pan Borneo Highway and headed straight to the checkpoint. A small, beautiful, road meandered along the mountain. Not long after, we reached the border. We parked our motorcycles in the shade and waited in the front of the checkpoint.

A short while later, the van arrived ... but by then the tour operator had disappeared.

Chapter 23 Special Ties with State Authorities

We could only sigh. The Malaysian checkpoint asked for the document that teve had talked about. Everyone just looked at each other not knowing what to say. he Malaysian checkpoint gave a clear answer -- the answer we already knew. Steve ad been saying all along, "Without the document, the motorcycles cannot cross, but eople can."

The tour operator did not answer our call, but communicated with us through VhatsApp, "Give me an hour. There is a restaurant in front of the checkpoint. Wait here." We went there to eat a little something and went back to wait at the checkpoint. But after an hour, nothing happened.

I was furious. So was Steve.

The rest of the group chose to look for a silver lining in this boring situation. They crossed the border into Indonesia to go shopping, get a massage, thinking that if hey couldn't take their motorcycles across, at least they got to do a little bit of ightseeing and take some pictures. I didn't go along with them. If I couldn't go with he badass Yellow, then I didn't want to go. We came together, so we would go ogether.

The tour company still told us to wait a little longer and that they were almost done. But by then Steve had already lost his patience. He didn't want to go to Indonesia nd neither did he wish to continue on with the tour company anymore. He decided to o his own way.

I had to have an answer for myself whether or not I should go with Steve.

I checked with the tour operator in Indonesia from the time I woke up. I asked my team in Chiang Mai to contact them for me. It was true that our tour company did contact them and they were ready to come and pick us up.

I had an answer for myself, "wait".

Steve walked over to the Triumph Tiger, furiously starting the engine. His headlights seemed wild and more menacing all of a sudden. Perhaps the motorcycle took after its master, spitting out the exhaust, roaring madly, eyebrows furrowed through the LED headlights, then dashed out of the checkpoint with exactly the same attitude as its master.

I lay waiting under a tree near the yellow Ducati, guarding over dozens of my friends' motorcycles.

Two hours had passed, my friends slowly crossed back from Indonesia. Most of them didn't think we would eventually be able to cross over, so they took pictures with the sign that said Indonesia, just in case.

Some people called the tour operator and still got the same answer, "Wait a little longer."

Three hours had passed. We sat and talked among ourselves, "We'd better get back. Don't think we can go. There's no document and they're not likely to get it."

"We should wait until the checkpoint closes. The tour company will have no excuse. Otherwise, they can tell us later that it's our fault that we didn't wait."

"If we can't cross over, we still have two more days for sightseeing in Kuching. No need to hurry."

So, everyone concluded that they would wait.

After three and a half hours, the tour company sent us a message that we read but no one believed, "Ready. Go ahead and cross."

We thought it wasn't possible, but we were wrong. The tour company really had a special connection with the state authorities. This was this company's strength. It took about twenty minutes on the Malaysian side, followed by over two hours on the Indonesian side, and we successfully brought ourselves and our motorcycles into Indonesia.

We had arrived at the checkpoint at 10:30 am and passed through the checkpoint at about sundown. If we were to reach Singkawang, we definitely would have to ride at night. Some of us had problems riding at night and one of them was me. Wherever the sunset is, I stay overnight there. "Please don't let me slow you down. Tomorrow, I'll leave early in the morning and I'm sure I can catch up."

Without the tour company, nothing was a problem. We all decided to go together and would stop to stay overnight in Sambas, which was almost 100 kilometers from the checkpoint. Google Map estimated that it would take almost two hours.

Shortly after the checkpoint, the four-lane road became a small road with no shoulders, wide enough to let cars pass. The smoothly paved road with no potholes took us toward a big mountain with dense forest, that is Borneo's charm. Riding was very enjoyable, curving back and forth in the high mountain, surrounded by first-class nature.

The roaring, badass exhaust sound was clearly heard. The moderate speed, and the lean angle needed to use the tires' rim surface which is softer than the center. My speed was between 60-100 kilometers per hour. This was a perfect combination for the two-cylinder, signature no-spring L-twin valve and tremendous torque Ducati Scrambler 1100. It was born for this.

The ad-hoc marshal, Resuan told me after we arrived at the hotel, "This road is so beautiful. It's the most beautiful part in this trip, and so much fun to ride, just like Nan Province in your country."

What?... I have this in my neighborhood?

What did I travel this far for?... Oh! Brother.

Chapter 24 A Wife Who May Come with the Darkness of Sambas

As soon as we entered the city, the road conditions did not change, but the riding condition did dramatically. There were many motorcycles on the road. Some riders came out of the alleys, some turned into their houses, some stopped to chat with others, and some parked to go do some shopping. Cars overtook motorcycles and came into our lane. Everything was chaotic. Worst yet, these bikes made abrupt turns without proper signals.

The speed came down to less than sixty kilometers per hour. It was like riding in Vietnam, except for less horn honking, and narrower streets thus giving the impression of being more chaotic. This was just a small town, but why was there so much confusion?

We arrived in Sambas just before sunset. The hotel looked like three connecting shophouses. The ground floor was open and expansive. The two top floors were guest rooms. The floor plan was done with no consideration for windows. Some thought we should go to stay in Singkawang because the hotels there would be much better. But most felt that riding in sunlight already felt chaotic and dangerous, riding at night didn't seem to be a good idea. Even if this was a one-star hotel, we thought it was a better choice. So, tonight we settled for Sambas.

After taking a shower, we went out to find something to eat. The sun had already set and it was completely dark. It had been a long day and we felt like walking over to eat rather than riding our motorcycles. So, we chose a restaurant near the hotel that was recommended by the receptionist. Everyone went there to eat but there was no vegetarian food.

A girl out of nowhere offered me a ride on her motorcycle to another place to eat, not far from the hotel. She was so shy and giggly throughout the ride. She was charming in her own way, but that charm was in no way alluring to me, so, I didn't cling to her waist or try to hold closer to her midriff.

The restaurant she took me to was non-descript, but next to it was a local pizza place. They could make vegetarian pizza and we were able to somewhat communicate. So, I told the girl that I was going to eat at the pizza place. She wanted to sit and keep me company. I told her that I would walk back by myself and for her not to worry and that she could go back. A young man in the restaurant saw a stranger and could tell that I was a tourist. So, he mustered enough courage to come over and talk. His name was Yuzril, and he could speak some English, enough for us to communicate. He looked like he was not older than twenty.

"My parents are farmers. I'm now old enough, so I came to the city to find work, so that I can send money home." It is the same trend across ASEAN countries. The young generation does not want to continue to work on the farms, or in the fields. Then he went on, "You are the first foreigner I have ever met." I was shocked and surprised, but thought that it might be possible. This is a new small town, small checkpoint, and riding a motorcycle into Indonesia is not easy.

"You speak English well," I said.

"I learned from Hollywood movies."

I thought to myself that this was an excellent way to learn English.

In fact, if Thai children learn English by watching Hollywood movies, with subtitles on, I would assume that the results would be better than studying under the Ministry of Education's curriculum. But they will be influenced by American culture and civilization, which I'm not sure whether this is a good or bad idea. We exchanged Instagram information, and up until now still 'like' each other's posts.

Before going to bed, the group got together for our own briefing on the next day's plan. Tuan Haji and the tour operator in Indonesia also sat in. Our tour company of sole-ownership, our troublemaker got off the van in Kuching and didn't come along, so the meeting went smoothly without any problems.

The group's opinion was divided into two. The first option was to follow the program and go to Pontianak, where we would ride our motorcycles across the Equator to earth's southern hemisphere on a joyful ride of 216 kilometers which Google Map said would take   four and a half hours.

The road would not be on tranquil mountains, but runs through several towns. Not much speed could be used and we had to be careful of cross traffic, turning vehicles, overtaking cars that would come into our lane and most of all, those motorcycles who turned before realizing that they had to look behind them too.

If we chose this route, the next day, we had to return to the checkpoint and ride to Kuching on a 413 kilometers route, which Google estimated to be over eight hours excluding the time needed at the checkpoint. Half of the group wanted to choose the first option, because riding a motorcycle across the Equator is a once-in-a-lifetime experience that doesn't come by that easily.

The other half thought differently. It was a disagreement without conflict. Without the tour operator, there were no problems. We laughed happily despite the difference of opinions. This group felt that we had been riding our motorcycles for several days. The planned tour program was not followed. We hardly got to do any sight-seeing, but to ride from town to town. The restaurants were terrible. The tour company only took us to cheap places to eat.

So, we should go only as far as Singkawang, making time for relaxing stops to take in the local Indonesian way of life, eat good food, and spend more time on leisurely travel. The distance was only 80 kilometers. We were already really tired. If we chose the first option, on our return day we had to ride for up to eight hours, excluding the time at the checkpoint. So, the verdict was option two.

As we concluded day seven of the journey, we hadn't reached our intended destination since we had wasted many hours at the checkpoint, but successfully crossed over to Indonesia. The total distance today was 202.9 kilometers. Before falling asleep, I thought it was lucky that I didn't cling to the girl's waist. Tonight, I hoped she wouldn't knock on my door with the proposition that we spend the night together. But if she did, my inspiration might work differently in the dark ... Brrrrrr.

Chapter 25 Happiness in the City of a Thousand Temples Like Chiang Mai Named Singkawang

The sun was shining. The members of our group, one by one, came down to their motorcycles shortly after seven o'clock. As if he could read my mind, Bob came over, prepared to spray mascara on the Ducati's chain. Tuan Haji gave a briefing before we left, "We will travel to Singkawang for a distance of only 80 kilometers, then we'll go have some coffee and then to our accommodation."

"Raj will be the lead rider today." Damn. "Raj rides slowly, and he has a map and GPS. And judging from how people drive around here, riding a bit more slowly would be good."

So, the Yellow Ducati got a chance to flaunt her badass sound in front of the procession at a maximum speed of 90 kilometers per hour and no more than 60 kilometers per hour when passing through the community areas. A straight, smoothly paved road, wide enough to let two cars pass, stretched ahead. There were no shoulders, or mountains. At a glance, the towns looked small but when we passed the community areas or the markets, we saw a lot of people and busy traffic.

Indonesia has a large population of 260 million. It is governed by a democratic political system. More than 80 percent of the population are Muslims. It is the country with the largest Muslim population in the world. Indonesia was a Dutch colony for about 300 years before Japan invaded the country and drove the Dutch out. Then Japan lost the war, so Indonesia declared independence. However, the Netherlands refused, wanting Indonesia back as their colony. So, they waged war, but the Netherlands lost.

161

And even when they lost, they refused to leave ... But because colonizatio with 'I-have-guns, you-have-swords, I-can-do-anything' mentality was wrong, man countries joined hands to pressure the Netherlands. They finally retreated and gav back the independence to Indonesia in 1949 but refused to let go of Papua territory This caused the conflict to accumulate over the years, just as England made Kashmi a land of conflict between India and Pakistan.

Today, Indonesia has its independence, with indie charm mixed with unique allure of Indonesian way of life. As gigantic, beautiful, and mighty motorcycles cruised by the markets, people turned to look, as we gazed at them. We noticed large crowds thronging in shops and markets. There were no shopping malls, no convenience stores, only small (small to medium) SME businesses. People looked vibrant. Trading was bustling, and there seemed to be more buyers than sellers. And I had a feeling that some didn't have enough goods to sell.

Peering around and reading from the way the Indonesians looked at us, I saw two expressions. One was a perplexed look – 'there are airplanes and public transportations. Why don't they take it? Why ride motorcycles to expose themselves to the sun and the wind?' kind of look; and the other was the look of motorcycle riders' who have certain attitudes that other people don't understand. It was a look of admiration, fascination, and desire to share quality time. It's an attitude that these are not just motorcycles but a craft for your soul -- the attitude that could be communicated just by an eye-contact.

We rode along in a long, orderly line, looking gracious and magnificent. We stopped to refuel before entering Singkawang. It seemed there were not enough pumps -- more buyers than sellers. Almost every pump had a line of cars, motorcycles, and wagons with lots of gallons waiting. Over tens of our motorcycles queued up to get gas. In fact, the tour company had to pay, but the guy didn't come, and of course he didn't give us any money.

We continued our journey and reached Singkawang a short while afterward. The city's most famous temple is the 'Tri Dhama Bumi Raya', built by Chinese Buddhists in 1878. It was hard to tell if this was a Buddhist temple or a shrine, but since they used the word Temple, let us assume so. One thing that Singkawang and

Chiang Mai have in common is the fact that they have so many temples so they are both called the "City of a Thousand Temples".

After visiting the temple, we went for coffee at a nearby coffee shop. It was an ordinary place in a shophouse. We sat there blissfully and relaxed. Even though the weather was a little too hot, it felt good. Today's itinerary was over. It was only ten o'clock in the morning, and the tour company was nowhere to be found.

The city's holy spirits must have thought that we needed more entertainment so a pair of musicians with acoustic guitars were sent to play for us Michael Bolton' hit, "Baby, you don't know what it's like. To love somebody, to love somebody." We sang in the cafe, with such joy brought by the acoustic guitars and the songs that coul delight people of all creeds equally. It was a memorable moment.

We stayed at a four-star hotel, located in the same area as the shopping mall Those who wanted to rest went straight there. Those who did not want to go to th hotel continued to do more sightseeing. We rode out to see Singkawang's beaches. Th fact that Singkawang had a beach gave it a tiny edge over Chiang Mai in my mind.

The spot where we drank refreshing coconut water and watched the sea was almost at the point marking the end of the island's longest stretch. There might be a slightly longer stretch on the island, but this point was at the end of the longest stretch throughout the 8 days that we had traveled with a distance of almost 2,600 kilometers from Hat Yai. It had been a great trip, great Ducati, great friends, awesome life, so this was an excellent coconut.

Just like Go Lung opined, "A person lives in the world. If he gets to do what he wants to do earnestly, should he be happy?"

Scanning the beach, I saw people who wanted to ride a motorcycle got to ride a motorcycle; those who wanted to travel by motorcycles, got to do so; and those who wanted to live a biker's lifestyle got to do so as well.

We got to do what we wanted. We should be happy... and we were happy.

Chapter 26 Kilometer Zero of the Pan Borneo Highway

Late that afternoon, I checked in at the four-star Swiss - Belinn Singkawang hotel and met an Indonesian receptionist, who I thought looked so ravishing, that I completely forgot all about the Sambas girls. The ability to control my wandering eyes reduced to nil. The eyes are the windows to the soul, and they were declaring independence from my brain. This woman's beauty was truly mesmerizing.

I didn't want to be a Samba son-in-law anymore, but resolved to be tied to Singkawang. I completely forgot about missing Nusara, and in fact, even forgot that I'm already married. Hmmm, perhaps my marriage certificate would not be valid here. My marital status became 'single' immediately. I asked to take her picture as a souvenir to take with me to Chiang Mai. She did not object and smiled beautifully. I pressed the shutter. Singkawang of Indonesia, the city of a thousand temples is no less than Chiang Mai at all.

There are thousands of temples like Chiang Mai. The women are as beautiful as Nusara like Chiang Mai.

After lingering at the check-in counter until everyone already went up to their room, I begrudgingly said goodbye to her and went up to my room. It was a wonderful room with a gorgeous view and excellent bed. I took a shower, lounged around for a while, then went down to find some coffee in the shopping mall that was connected to the hotel.

I saw Thai writings in the shopping mall. A tea shop opened here, serving authentic Thai tea and Thai coffee with tea leaves and coffee beans imported from

Thailand, but the owner was Indonesian. The shop is called Dum Dum (pronounced Duem Duem') Thai Drinks.

For dinner, I saw an Italian restaurant in the hotel, so I didn't go out with my friends. To conclude day 8 of the trip, the total distance today was 119.3 kilometers. As I was getting ready to go to bed, my mind drifted to the spellbinding receptionist of Singkawang. Hmmm ... Should I remain in this town for another ten years? Before I went to bed, Nusara called to confirm that she would arrive the next day and would see me in Kuching. She probably sensed some risk to her marital state.

The next morning was day nine of the journey. We, motorcycle lovers who thrive on living on those two wheels, gradually came to do the vehicle check. As usual, Bob, the van driver, took care of the Yellow Ducati's final transmission kit sprockets chain.

For today's route, we would backtrack through Sambas and go through the Indonesian checkpoint to enter Malaysia and end the trip at a hotel on the river bend in Kuching.

An Indonesian government official came to wave the flag. I wasn't sure who he was, maybe the mayor of this city. When everyone was ready, the flag was waved we dashed off out of Singkawang at high speed. The police choppers were blasting the sirens that could be heard all over the city at every intersection. The Yellow Ducati was designated to lead the procession because she has the lowest speed. Tuan Haji wanted to avoid all kinds of problems here.

We stopped for gas in Sambas and had to wait in a long line as usual. Then we continued our journey through the winding road that traversed the big mountain. There were hardly any cars much like the day we arrived. The distance was about 80 kilometers. After leaving the gas station, we all went at our own speed, no longer in a procession.

Some just rode casually to take in the perfect nature on the mountain, invoking blissful feelings in the heart. Some stopped to photograph the scenic beauty along the way.

But some rode at lightning speed, blasting reverberating roars from their exhaust pipes echoing across the road, dashing through the greenery.

Fu and Philip unleashed the horses down into their BMW wheels and zoomed by at a breakneck speed that could rip your soul apart. The thunderous sound from the Boxers was subtle yet powerful, punctuated by the sound of the six-cylinder, inline engine of the 24-valve-1600cc BMW sounding like a full orchestra that was fading into the Indonesian horizon.

We arrived at the checkpoint at almost the same time. Passing through the checkpoints on both the Indonesian and the Malaysian sides was efficient and swift. It only took less than half an hour for the whole procession.

After this, there were two options -- either returning to our hotel in Kuching or going to see the kilometer zero post of the pan Borneo highway via a new road leading to one village that is difficult to access. It is almost at the tip of the Malaysian peninsula near Tanjung Datu National Park. The newly-finished road was smooth, beautiful, and grand. It ended at a roundabout and the kilometer zero sign, next to the sign for the beach and the ocean.

A small road from the checkpoint took us to the Pan Borneo Highway. The first option was to turn right into Kuching. The second option was to turn left, heading towards the beach at kilometer zero. I chose to turn left onto the Pan Borneo Highway stretch that was under construction and had got rained on. The ride was a mix of stress and fun. And then came the last stretch of the road which was now completed and it was truly mankind's triumph over God.

The smooth road meandered through the mountain. The trees were green and lush. The weather was pleasant. This was the true perfection and charm of the man-made Pan Borneo Highway that enabled the God-given beauty of Borneo to be revealed.

With the appropriate speed for each motorcycle and the individual person's spirit, it didn't take us long. We took a picture with the sign -- the picture which the tour company later used to publish in a local newspaper. Then we traveled through the Pan Borneo Highway stretch that was under construction, back to Kuching.

The trip had been completed. We checked into the hotel, I took a shower, and relaxed.

At the party tonight, the tour company prepared to present everyone with a certificate for taking part in the 2,388-kilometers motorcycle trip in Borneo. I didn't go according to the program being fed up with the quarrelsome atmosphere which I assumed would definitely recur.

I took a Grab to the airport. Nusara disembarked the plane with a helmet in hand, swaying left and right, prettier than the young receptionist in Singkawang. Love is blind. But the separation from one's better half for more than ten days also added restlessness. We embraced each other lovingly and felt how much we longed to be close to each other.

Her dismissive 'go-far-away' mood completely disappeared. Hand-in-hand we took another Grab back to the hotel. Along the way, I said to her, "Nusara, let's go to Kuching," she smiled timidly.

Part 3: Self Ride

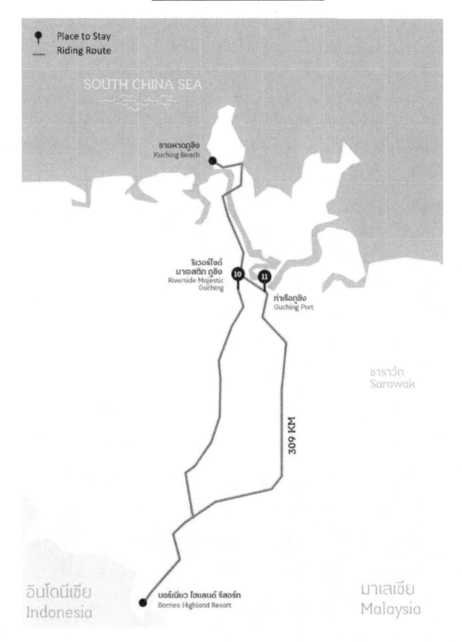

Chapter 27 A Mecca for Motorcycle Lovers

The tour program in Borneo would end this morning. The last activity was to ship the motorcycle back to Port Klang in Kuala Lumpur. We rode together as a group. The round seat on top of the two exhaust pipes with a badass sound had Nusara sitting on it. It was the perfection of life in a way. After riding leisurely and enjoying the surrounding for a while, we fell back out of the procession. But it was fine, we had already pinned our destination.

The tour operator and the transport company met to hand over the motorcycle. I asked when the ship would leave, and if it would be possible for me to do a sightseeing ride in Kuching with Nusara for a few more days. The transport company said the cut-off time was eleven o'clock the next day. Nusara and I said goodbye to everyone. Most of them would fly back that night. Some were staying on to continue with their own programs.

We started the Ducati and headed to Kuching's famous beach as suggested by TripAdvisor. Then, while heading back into town we happened to pass by the Sikh Temple there. So, we stopped to pray to the Scripture.

God took good care of us. We got to eat vegetarian food to our heart's content.

The love of the two-wheeled engineering is like a deadly virus that once you contract it, you will not be cured -- a virus that does not care about race, religion, sex, or age, had arrived in the Sikh temple of Kuching.

The Sikhs arrived in Kuching when the White Rajah named Brooke ruled Sarawak. The pictures in the temple also depicted Sikhs who were traffic policemen, all elegantly dressed up and donning turbans on their heads, standing next to a vintage motorcycle whose shape is adored by many.

The virus must have been spreading for a long time since the time of the White Rajah until it infected 'Mr. Dewlip' whom we met at the Sikh Temple. Mr. Dewlip was about sixty years old. He had recently retired and has been living a happy life after retirement going golfing and motorcycling. He owned a Kawasaki W800 with 800cc inline, two-cylinder engine and a Triumph Tiger, an 800cc inline three-cylinder engine motorcycle as well.

Kuching Traffic Police with Gurbachan Singh Akhara and Arjan Singh Cheema

That afternoon, him and his wife, on the Tiger, volunteered to take us on a jo ride on Kuching's scenic route that is famous among local bikers. We left the town c Kuching via highway 1119 then Q1179. We headed toward a majestic mountain. Th elevation gain reminded me of the road going up Doi Inthanon. The temperatur continued to drop.

The route was breathtaking. If we don't count the small meandering loc: roads in Indonesia and the last stretch of the Pan Borneo Highway near kilometer zer that was just finished, this was the most beautiful road on this trip. We stopped to tak pictures in front of the Borneo Highlands Resort sign, then we took a small roa number 1123 heading to the Indonesian border.

As a matter of fact, if the tour company had planned for us to enter Indonesi through this side of the border, we would have saved two full hours on the road. Loc: people also use this route to get to Pontianak, the city on the Equator which we ha intended to ride across, but did not manage to.

One must have the love of motorcycling to understand which roads are wort seeing. The two-wheeled soulcraft created a bond between us regardless of age. I fact, any kind of differences is not a problem. Perhaps motorcycle lovers may start revolution and declare an independence, nullify all borders, and abolish all forms o regimes, leaving only motorcycle riding to various places, and call it an 'absolut motorcycle monarchy' regime. People may be much happier.

We bonded instantly, while chatting and drinking coffee happily. Ou friendship continued to blossom. The next morning, Mr. Dewlip took us to eat vegetarian meal that was both delicious and inexpensive. The total price for thre people came to only around 3-4 Ringgit.

Then he led us to drop off the yellow Ducati at the port. We said goodbye and Mr. Dewlip promised to make his dream come true at our next meeting.

People who love motorcycling in Malaysia, either East or West can be divided into two groups -- Those who have already fulfilled their dreams by riding on this road; and those who dream of riding on this road before they die.

It's the Mecca of Malaysian motorcycle lovers.

This road is not in Malaysia, not in Brunei, not in Indonesia.

Not in Laos, not in Cambodia, not in Myanmar or Vietnam, not in Europe.

Not in India, and not in America.

But it's in Thailand.

It is the infamous road with 1,864 curves, 350 kilometers long - Highway 108

Connecting Chiang Mai, Hod, Mae Sariang, Khun Yuam, and

Mae Hong Son.

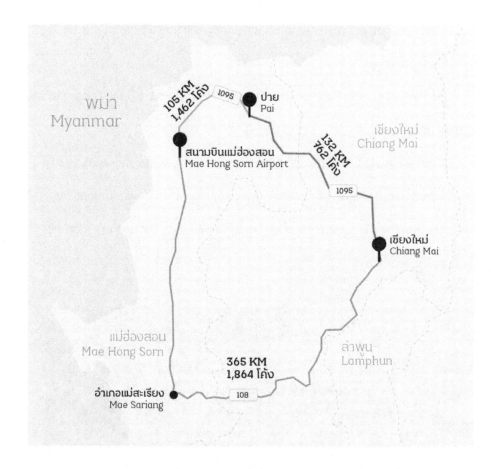

This is a dream road of every Malaysian motorcycle lovers that I have met, including Mr. Dewlip - A Sikh man with a beard as lush and beautiful as a lion's mane.

"I'm going this year. I'm going to fulfill my dreams on the 1,864-curve highway," he continued.

"I don't have a ride mate yet. My family would be very worried if I were to ride alone. "

"Okay, if you are really going, I will ride with you all the way from Kuala Lumpur."

He looked gratified and contemplative. He realized that the chance to fulfill his dream just increased.

After we parted, Nusara and I continued our trip to the museum, where we discovered that Kuching of Sarawak is a city with an awe-inspiring history. Its history came from a hipster -- not any ordinary hipster, but one of the same calibers as Lu Xiaofeng!

Chapter 28 The Hipster Rajah and His Hipster State

The word 'hipster' has many meanings according to various schools of thought. The definition that I think best fits one Englishman is 'having advanced political thinking and own lifestyle'. -- A not so ordinary dream of the hipster named James Brooke.

"Is it possible for me to sail my ship on the water that has never been touched by any European bilge and recorded in the history as possible?"

In 1839, hipster James Brooke sailed the first European ship to Borneo and Kuching.

Everyone knows how much fun God has in piecing together stories. And His method is known to be mysterious and astonishing. With hipster James, God did not spare him. He granted him an event that made James Brooke shine as a hipster in Sarawak.

God granted one event four years before hipster James sailed to Sarawak. In 1835, Sarawak was ruled by Brunei, and a rebellion erupted that year. Hipster James arrived in Sarawak in 1839 and his arrival led the Sultan to use him as an agent to suppress the rebellion, (or to make it fit the present day, we can call it 'outsourcing for rebellion suppression), with an agreement that if the mission was successful, hipster James would rule Sarawak.

Two years later, hipster James gained the rulership of Sarawak. And seven years after his arrival he was appointed the first White Rajah of the region -- whom would like to call Hipster Rajah James.

His account is exhibited in The Brooke Gallery at Fort Margherita, a wonderful museum located on the banks of the Sarawak River, across from the city. It has a gun turret on the roof.

Hipster Rajah James was an Englishman. And although England has the nobles, courtiers and the hierarchy of ranks and titles, the Rajah did not like to act that way. It seemed that he didn't even like the aristocratic system. He ruled Sarawak during the time when the Sultans and Rajahs in this region adhered strictly to their customs. The people could not look at the king's face, and everything, even the heads of the people, were considered belonging to the Rajahs.

But Hipster Rajah James acted like a government by the people and for the people. If he had set up a political party, it might have had a slogan like 'Think anew. Act anew.' or a beautiful future in orange hue (translator's note: The author refers to the Future Forward political party of Thailand).

A country that increases tax by economic expansion is considered to be skillfully managed, but, a country that increases taxation by increasing tax is considered to be managed with a lack of skill. The tax measure is a known benchmark of administrative skill.

And without doubt, Hipster Rajah James ruled the country with skill.

Despite suffering from the plundering of the trading fleet, and threats from the surrounding states, Hipster Rajah did not rule with too big an army, nor acquire submarines to build his stability. So, when the state did not have too much expense, there was no need to collect high tax.

Hipster Rajah James ruled under economics principles, i.e. giving every tribe and every state freedom to trade in peace and under clear laws. Only this could make people wealthy, instead of expanding the territory using military force, weapons, and prowess to occupy, or even leak fake news to spread fear in order to subjugate the people.

Instead, he expanded by way of economic power, peace and justice, enabling Sarawak to expand the territory vastly during the reign of Hipster Rajah James and continued to do so until the following reigns.

The succeeding White Rajah issued 9 rules that still remain in effect up until this day. They are modern and just rules that spread the hipsterism down to the city, to people and to the citizens of Sarawak.

This museum gave us a better understanding of Sarawak, so much so that I didn't want to call it the State of Sarawak or just a city -- the words that have become clichés. Calling it 'Hipster Sarawak' was more like how I felt. It's a new definition of Malaysia that I use only for myself.

Malaysia consists of twelve states, three federal territories, and Hipster Sarawak.

I'm not sure if this violates their national security law, but let's assume that I call it this way with a good intention and maintain full respect for the hipster characters of Sarawak.

In the late afternoon, Nusara and I took a cruise down the Sarawak River, the major river of Kuching. Looking at the city on the river banks, Kuching is a charming, simple and beautiful city.

There was a performance from different tribes, and concluded with a view of the sunset from the boat. It was so romantic we felt as if we were on another honeymoon -- the 37th time, if I remembered correctly. And this does not include the times when Nusara wanted me to 'go far away', after we started the trips.

The next day, we flew to Kuala Lumpur, and then directly from Kuala Lumpur to our beloved Chiang Mai. We returned to Chiang Mai on Tuesday. I had an appointment to pick up my motorcycle at Port Klang on Wednesday of the following week. I would have time to relax, and sort out all my work, with a peace of mind in Chiang Mai for a week.

But the tranquil peace of mind lasted only two days, because on Thursday, the tour company decided to hold the yellow Ducati hostage and call for a ransom of 2,300 Ringgit.

Part 4: Runaway Ride

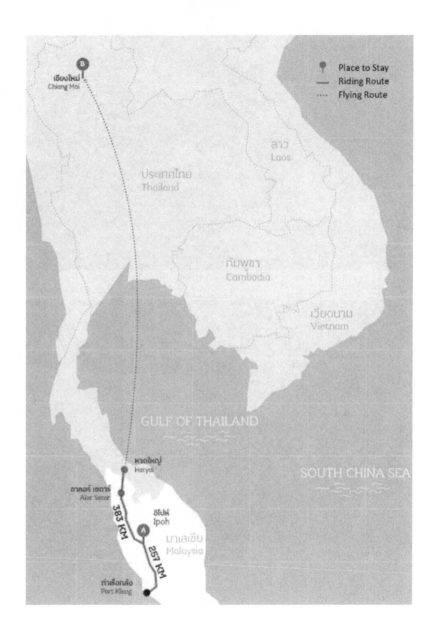

Chapter 29 The Yellow Motorcycle was Held for Ransom

The tour company threatened that if I did not transfer 2,300 Ringgit to them, they would keep the Yellow Ducati at the port and send it back to Kuching to be stored in their private warehouse. The threat was sent through both group and personal WhatsApp chats.

The reason? Because I didn't want to send them the pictures from the Huawei Muay Thai Tom Yum especially the photos from Indonesia. The company wanted to post them on their Facebook page to promote their upcoming trip to China.

I wasn't going to send them. They hadn't gone along with us, nor had they paid for our meals or gas. There was no service car, nor marshal. We didn't get to go on most of the advertised excursions. The promises in the brochure hadn't been delivered at all. And to think that they still had the nerve to ask for the photos that we have had so much fun taking to advertise themselves as professional tour organizers…

All my friends helped me lambast them -- that those are my pictures, and the company had no right whatsoever to use them. So, they changed the reason to the fact that I was the reason why everybody went to Labuan, and it had cost them 2,300 Ringgit extra.

So, my friends said, "Everybody went together. We all had to chip in. How can you charge Raj alone?"

Then they changed the reason again, saying the Ducati was going at lightning speed. So, the police slapped them with a fine of 2,300 Ringgit.

My friends said, "Then, we all should have gotten it, because we were all riding together in a group, almost always."

"In fact, the one least likely to get fined is Raj's yellow Ducati, because whenever we raced, he often couldn't catch up."

Eventually, the tour company chose the Labuan island reason to hold the yellow Ducati for 2,300 Ringgit ransom.

And they did what they do best -- changed the subject, kicked me out of the WhatsApp group and sent me a private message, "Transfer the money before noon, Tuesday and pick up the motorcycle on Wednesday. Transfer the money and don't contact me again. I'll block you after this message."

My friends and I had our own WhatsApp group, so I know from them what was going on and about the pick-up schedule for their vehicles, which the tour company moved to Monday at 2:00 p.m. without telling me. Nusara was packing my bag to get ready for the flight to Malaysia. My father prepared the ransom of 2,300 Ringgit, neatly tucked in an envelope and said, "Don't you get into any disagreement overseas."

I took it, and prostrated myself at his feet. I persuaded Nusara to go with me. She hastily packed and we were going to look for plane tickets at the airport.

"Even if we pay, it won't be over. They will blackmail me again." I thought to myself while sitting on the plane.

My friend gave words of encouragement that the shipping fees should be about 700 Ringgit per vehicle. The motorcycle belonged to me and the receipt was with me. Once I had paid the fees, it should be over, they couldn't withhold my vehicle.

But I had seen quite a bit of the tour company's ability to leverage the power of state authorities, and it worried me. In particular, the astonishing strings that they were able to pull at the immigration checkpoint on the way out of Malaysia to

Indonesia was definitely not just ordinary strings. The Malaysians still couldn't believe that they pulled it off. The mayor of almost all of the cities that we passed through came to dine with us and wave the flag. We also got police escort in and out of town. What if they came to pick a fight with us at Bukit Kayu Hitam, or at Sadao checkpoint?

Confusing thoughts kept pouring from my unsettling mind. The phone rang at the airport. My older brother called, "I know a prosecutor in Malaysia, in Kuala Lumpur. Do you want to dine with him?" I felt better. "I already called him. He asked me if you had done anything illegal. If not, then you don't have to worry. But if you feel uneasy, or have any problems, you can call or dine with him." My older brother's strong connection to people in high places is also second to none in the land and also expanded continuously to Malaysia.

My plane landed at Kuala Lumpur Airport on a late Sunday night. We stayed at Tune Hotel at the airport. The next morning, Raman, the owner of the blue Yamaha Ténéré 1200 arrived from Penang and took us on a bus from the airport to Port Klang. The tour company arranged for everyone (except me) to pick up their motorcycles at 2:00 p.m., but we arranged to meet among ourselves first before 11:00 a.m.

We got ready, rehearsed, and were prepared to abduct the hostage, the badass Yellow Ducati. Of course, I brought my spare keys. When we arrived at the shipping company, we found that it was not hidden or stored elsewhere, but parked with other motorcycles. I felt a bit better.

The shipping company indicated that all the vehicles had arrived safely and for us to bring our receipts and present them to Accounting. Accounting would verify the documents and payment. If everything was in order, we could take the vehicles and leave.

We took turns submitting the documents. They all checked out but not even a single Ringgit had been paid, because the tour company had not made a transfer to the shipping company.

Chapter 30 Not Only was the Yellow Motorcycle Held for Ranson

One hour had passed. The shipping company and the tour company were in contact with each other. The invoice total was over 7,000 Ringgit. The tour company transferred the amount 2,300 Ringgit less and said that the remaining amount could be collected from Raj, the owner of the Yellow Ducati.

All my Malaysian-motorcycle-enthusiasts friends agreed that this was not any individual person's fault. The tour company was haggling with all of us. We had ten motorcycles there, so we should divide the expense among everybody which came to 230 Ringgit each.

I stood up and said, "The tour company is harassing just me, and this has nothing to do with you guys. Here, my dad already gave me the money."

But all of my friends insisted that "They don't want to harass just you. They know that you are from Thailand, and they can threaten you. Just pay 230 Ringgit like everyone else."

Nusara and I could feel the bond of friendship that had been formed throughout the trip -- the friendship born out of spending quality time together on the roads with breathtaking scenery on those beautiful islands atop spectacular motorcycles.

Another hour had passed, the money still wasn't in the account. So, we went out for lunch. Having a chance to talk, we found that all had suffered a fair share of deceit. It was such a mess. Some of them had intended to travel with their wives and paid for two. The tour company postponed the trip. This was their first trip alone without their wives and they did not get the money back

Many paid for the trip to China, which would take place in the next six months. Most recently, the trip got postponed for a full thirteen months. That's right -- one year and one month without refunds. The plan is subject to change without prior notice. Everyone had to pay about 100 Malaysian Ringgit toll fee to get into Indonesia. No one received any reimbursement from the tour company.

The tour company had problems with everyone. They collected the money from everyone, avoided paying the expense that was supposed to be included in the package, and were extremely confident in their connection with the state authorities. The level of confidence that they expressed was so inflated as if they had Mahathir's power in their hands.

Some of us brought a formal complaint to be signed and sent to the Malaysian Consumer Protection Bureau. Everyone signed without hesitation.

Having finished our lunch, we went back to the shipping company, thinking that the money would have been deposited by then -- but we were wrong. We were too optimistic. The accounting department of the motorcycle shipping company said the money still had not been deposited. Some of us checked with the bank. They were advised that it might take up to 24 to 48 hours before the money could be credited.

It was okay for those living near Port Klang. They could just go home and come back the next day. But it was not quite all right for those coming from afar, such as Kelantan, Penang or Chiang Mai, who had to find accommodation for the night. The additional cost was not included in the tour package. We had to pay for that out of our own pockets.

Although many of them were from Kuala Lumpur, they had to take leave from their work –and yet the tour company couldn't care less. They were certain about their readily-accessible, strong ties with the state authorities. Who would have thought that in today's world, in which the truth can be exposed on the Internet, there's someone who still dares to do this?

But the tour company was even more conniving. They used Facebook in marketing and posted our photos that were taken with the Huawei Tom Yum Kung camera on their personal Facebook page. They did not open it as a business page, so, there are no ratings, nor reviews, and undesirable comments are deleted immediately.

Steve wrote a comment on their Facebook page: "I joined a tour with this company and want to warn people thinking of joining their tours. They are unprofessional, inexperienced, and fraudulent." In less than five minutes, everything disappeared. He tried to keep posting, sometimes at midnight, sometimes at three a.m., but as soon as the sun came up, everything vanished.

Another two hours had passed.

Our opinions were split into two. The first group didn't want to wait any longer. They wanted to just pay and take their motorcycles, which means we each had to pay an additional 500 Ringgit. The second group said we should wait. If we couldn't take the vehicles the next day, we could still pay.

Finally, it was concluded that the shipping company should clear this matter with the tour company. We would ride our motorcycles out right then and there.

The shipping company insisted on 'no money come, no motorcycles go' round. We gave them an ultimatum -- these are our motorcycles and we will file a olice report. The shipping agent consulted the manager, the manager consulted accounting, Accounting consulted the bank. No one wanted any trouble or to make a ig deal out of it. Eventually, the shipping company notified us that, "Okay, you can o whatever you see fit, but we cannot release the motorcycles without the payment."

So, we set off to the police station.

Chapter 31 Win a Million from Gambling, and We'll Buy a (Damn) New Motorcycle

All motorcycles were detained. Everyone was now in the same boat. We ha all been poisoned by the tour company. But whenever we were together, we alway had belly laughs with one another.

The police station was a small building similar to our police stations bac home, with a spacious parking lot in front, but parking was prohibited. We came i with 4-5 cars, and all had to keep moving our vehicles out of the no-parking zone. W went in to file the police report. There was a female police officer wearing a hijab. Sh had large eyes, prominent nose, and fair skin -- very attractive. I looked at her an compared her with Nusara.

I walked over to Nusara and told her, "You're more beautiful than tha policewoman," then went back and continued to admire the beautiful policewoman.

We had finished filing the police report, and everybody signed. We took group photo in front of the police station, then went our own separate ways.

Philip, the owner of BMW K-1600, who showed up today in his BMW X5 persuaded Nusara and I to go with him, along with Tum, Helen and Fu. They sense our tension before we arrived, and tried to give us special treatment taking care of u as if we were state visitors. He took us to eat an excellent vegetarian meal in Por Klang, then to check into the same hotel as Fu.

Before leaving, he asked tentatively, "Shall we go to Genting tonight?"

Genting Highlands is where the largest casino in Malaysia is, with an observation deck, a shopping mall and an amusement park all in one area. I didn't think we were very close to Genting. He must be joking. So, I answered playfully, "Let's."

We took a shower and got some rest at the hotel, then went out for a walk. Then, Philip and his young and beautiful wife came to pick up Fu, me and Nusara in his BMW X5.

In the car, I asked Philip, "Are all of your wheels BMW?"

"Yes, they are powerful and makes me feel like a teenager."

Philip gave a good answer and he also drove like a real teenager -- soaring past all the cars and leaving them behind -- at the speed that BMW is good at ... high speed.

We arrived at Tum and Helen's house shortly, and switched to his splendid, spacious and comfortable Hyundai H1. We rode together all in one car.

Tum was in his sixties, but he looked younger than his age. Perhaps it was his constant living on the two-wheels that prevented him from aging. He seemed to enjoy a family life and life on the road.

"Are we really going to Genting?" I asked out of the blue.

I'm not sure whether Tum or Fu answered, "Do you think we're the tour company?" We howled with laughter. Evidently, we were really going to Genting.

The road going up to Genting was similar to the Hang Dong - Samoeng - Mae Rim road for motorcycle lovers in Chiang Mai.

"If you come on the weekend, you'd see a lot of motorcycles riding up," explained Tum.

It was understandable. A winding road meandering up a large mountain, gradually elevating, "Even Starbucks here, are also designed for bikers", he pointed out. "You get a discount here, if you come by motorcycle."

At an approximate elevation of 1,800 meters above sea level, the temperature continued to drop as we gained height. Rain was drizzling and fog was billowing. It was about 10pm now, pitch dark and beautiful. We were all missing our motorcycles.

The tour company created an uncomfortable situation that made us feel controlled, our heart squeezed. I didn't feel good. No one felt good.

So, we tried to find new options.

"I have a plan. So, we don't have to go to the port or deal with the tour company again tomorrow."

No one wanted to go to the pier, to sit and wait for hours on end, without any exact timeframe when we could get back our motorcycles, so we all paid attention to this plan.

"Tonight, we will win about a million. Tomorrow, we can to buy new motorcycles at the showroom." And we burst out laughing as usual.

I think we must have reached the mountain top. The weather was nice and cool, and foggy. There were gazillion, enormous hotels here, combined with shopping malls -- it felt like being in Las Vegas.

Tum showed us around like a local. The buildings here are enormous and inter-connected, so much so that, if you don't know your way around, you may need to consult Google Maps to find your way out. He led us into the casino, with dazzling ghts. People strived to win, tables full of money. Cigarette smell filled the air and shed in with every breath. There were card games, roulette, and the absolutely dispensable, slot machines.

Fu pointed something out to me. I had never noticed this before. "Raj, look. one of the gamblers here look happy."

When I looked, it was just like Fu said. The lights were supposed to bring yfulness, and the decor was to entertain, but people's facial expressions were neither yful nor entertained. They seemed to be suffering in their hearts and their face said all. "That's why I don't like to gamble," Fu said.

We continued on through to a large department store. There was a giant musement park inside. Dazzling lights abound. It was already 11pm, but the place as still crowded with young children, older kids, teenagers, adults, young-at-heart dults, and adults who still wanted to be teenagers -- people of all ages who did not eep.

Then we headed back. The temperature outside the building was now 20 egrees Celsius. It was drizzling.

We felt our bond strengthened. The mutual friendship of the Thais of Indian escent and the Malaysians of Chinese descent was blossoming in the car. We arrived ack at the hotel quite late at night. Philip said, "Tomorrow, once you get the notorcycles out, I will pick you up."

I didn't know what time we'd be able to get our motorcycles tomorrow. Maybe /e would, maybe we wouldn't. Maybe we would have to go back to the police station, r be coerced into paying more ...

Chapter 32 Pretty Horrid Beachside Road

The next morning, while we were thinking about going out for breakfast, a message popped up in the WhatsApp group chat at around ten o'clock. "You can pick up your motorcycles now." Philip replied almost immediately. Even his text message was like a BMW -- full of speed. "Coming to pick you up. Arriving shortly."

Picking up the motorcycles was quick and easy. In just ten minutes, we were freed from the shipping and tour companies. My friends invited Nusara and me to extend our stay for a few more days to go sightseeing, in order to end the trip on the high note. But, having witnessed the strong relationship between the tour company and immigration, Nusara and I were still ill at ease. They might hatch some other schemes to blackmail us some more or cause us more troubles. We wanted to leave Malaysia as soon as possible, so we departed immediately. The yellow Ducati was glowing exuberantly on the road freely, the way it should be.

Once freed from colonial rule, Malaysia took off on exceptionally high speed and has been shining brightly on the world stage. The same applied to India, Singapore, Indonesia and the Ducati that once freed from detention, it dashed beamingly on E1 Highway at a high speed. From 120 kilometers per hour, it accelerated to 130-140 kilometers per hour and hovered around there, while the overtaking speed sometimes reached 170 kilometers per hour.

It continued to soar, satisfying its master and Nusara.

The light-weight Yellow Ducati Scrambler 1100, at the speed under 120 kilometers per hour, was perfect, easily handled, fluid, fun and melodious.

At a greater speed, it felt a little too light, and I was not confident to do so. But today, its performance over 120 km was perfect because there was Nusara sitting in the back.

I was happy to finally decide to own it, after spending nearly a year choosing. As soon as it arrived at the showroom in Chiang Mai, I summoned the Yellow Ducati to my garage instantly. It was a great decision.

Today, we just aimed for the Thai border. We'd decide where to stay later when it got dark. Then, it started to rain and then it poured, and poured. After several days of apprehension, neither of us wanted to stop.

The yellow Ducati soared through the rain, piercing through the wind. Nothing could stop our joy of soaring. The sun was on the horizon, we turned off the E1 Highway heading to Ipoh, the capital of Perak. We stopped to refill the tank, and pour water out of our drenched shoes, booked a hotel and checked in, showered, sat back and relaxed and then went out for Italian food.

We went to the restaurant where the condiments were placed in a cuddling position on tables with a romantic ambiance. I came here during my last Singapore trip and ate alone thinking of Nusara. This time, I brought her with me. We sat at the same table, where the condiments still cuddled. The food tasted as delicious as before but I was not lonely this time. After dinner, we strolled down Ipoh's Walking Street and went back to the hotel.

Today was the first day of the journey after the tour program ended. We gained 257 kilometers of distance.

The next morning, we ate breakfast at the hotel, and went to pray to the Holy Scripture at the Sikh Temple of Ipoh for blessings, and set off, then stopped for lunch in Alor Setar, the birth place of Mahathir. Then we headed to the Thai border using the R152 local road. Judging from the map, it ran alongside the beach, and should be beautiful.

The experience of riding along the beach never let us down. We arrived shortly nd rode along the beach just how we wanted. A majestic flock of birds glided longside the beach, and our motorcycle. We were thinking about finding a spot to oak up the atmosphere, but something happened.

"*Hia*! (Damn!)." Dashing out from the side of the road, was not a car or a notorcycle that normally would make us swear unintentionally, "*Hia* (Damn)!", but it /as a Komodo dragon[17] that we called in Thai, "*Hia*" -- the name that has been used s a swear word. So, to be grammatically correct, one had to exclaim, "*Hia* (Damn)! ... *Hia* (Komodo dragon)!"

Komodo dragons are not like chicken, they don't turn around.

They are not like pigs on the roadside that are visible from afar.

They are not like the familiar and cute dogs.

Komodo dragons are not like goats that live a slow life, moving in slow notion, and when they cross the road, they don't dash out. They just occupy the whole rea.

Komodo dragons are something else.

Instinctively, hitting the brakes was not likely to work, speeding past it might /ork. It was a good, accurate instinct. The Komodo dragon cut in the rear of the)ucati. It did not turn around. It did not stop and panic. It had its own clear path -- its *hia* (damn)" own path.

My instinct also told me that the idea of soaking up the atmosphere, and taking)ictures, might not be such a good one. I still trusted my instincts. The three of us ;lided in the breeze along the beach. On the left was the beauty of the sea, the wind /aves, the free-flying birds. On the right was a grove of woods from which a couple

221

more Komodo dragons dashed out for us to see, giving a weird sensation on this R15 road.

Let's just say that if I were to name this road, it would be a 'Damn (*Hic* beautiful road along the beach'.

From the damn (*hia*) beautiful road along the beach, we got back onto E Highway that took us straight onto Bukit Kayu Hitam checkpoint, or commonly know in our country, the Sadao checkpoint. Before we could connect the dots betwee running into a Komodo dragon and a bad omen, and a few Komodo dragons migh mean a very bad omen telling us not to pass through immigration checkpoint today we already arrived.

Chapter 33 Riding a Motorcycle Nearby to Please a Woman

If there was going to be a problem, it would be here. We were well prepared to get through the checkpoint. The tour company has a strong connection with the state, we also have a connection with God. As far as I know, Islam is the national religion of Malaysia, which means that God is above the authority of the state in this country. Apart from having complete documentation, we left the rest to pure magic.

We asked everyone we know, especially Nusara's parents, to pray for us. They pray and meditate a lot. Whenever I want something, I always go and ask them to pray to the Prophet for me. We were fully taking advantage of our existing connections. We were confident in our magic, but if it failed, we could still contact the prosecutor in Kuala Lumpur, my brother's personal connection.

If we didn't count a few Komodo dragons we saw minutes earlier, our confidence ran high. We parked in front of the checkpoint, prepared the documents both for us and the motorcycle. Then, metaphorically, I snatched my sword out of its sheath, a long sword that could stab straight through the heart, and immediately headed into the Bukit Kayu Hitam checkpoint.

There were a few cars. The yellow Ducati was rolling along in the motorcycle lane, and stopped at a window. I didn't have to get off, or take off my helmet. I handed my passport to the officer, and had my fingers scanned. If there was to be a problem, it would be at this point and because of me, since the vehicle was under my name, and the copy of the passport in the tour company's hand was mine. But the officer stamped the passport with a smile.

Next, it was Nusara's turn. She handed her passport, and had her fingers scanned. She didn't have to get off the motorcycle or take off her helmet either. Then I heard Nusara saying "Thank you" and we were done at the Malaysian side and headed to Thailand.

Magic and well-prepared documents got us out of Malaysia successfully. We entered Sadao checkpoint, parked our motorcycle and went to line up in the passport stamp queue, then had our motorcycle checked at customs. After just a short while, we entered Thailand. We stopped for a cold drink, and to cool off in an air-conditioned room at McDonald's in front of Sadao Checkpoint, to make an official announcement.

"The hostage rescue mission is successful, with no damage to the hostage," I messaged everybody in Malaysia and Thailand.

At first, Nusara and I thought we'd ride home. It might take three to four days. But after crossing over, we agreed to go home in two days. The pickup truck I used to transport the badass yellow Ducati before would come to pick it up here, load it, and return straight to Chiang Mai. The guy named Man managed to find parking for us while waiting for the pickup truck, at the Yamaha center in Hat Yai, and he drove us to the airport. We flew directly from Hat Yai to Chiang Mai and arrived home that same evening.

My friends in Malaysia and I are still chatting through WhatsApp. They're aiming to make this tour company stop scamming other motorcycle enthusiasts or organizing these sub-par events and programs in such an unethical manner.

Sabideen, the head honcho of Sarawak, the same state as the tour company, made an appointment with the State Tourism Board to question why they allowed such an unethical tour operator to use their logo as endorsement, and even promote their events on the Sarawak Tourism Board's website. Some planned to fight the tour company through the Consumer Protection Bureau.

While I was writing this book, the tour company continued to promote their trips to China and Bali on their Facebook account that showed no comments, or reviews. Most recently, in less than two weeks before departure date, they just announced that the trip to China had been postponed from August to September of the following year... a thirteen-months postponement.

Four or five days later, the yellow Ducati disembarked from the back of the pickup truck safe and sound. Almost immediately, its master and Nusara started the engine and took a joy ride around our beloved Chiang Mai city.

I was relaxed, peaceful and happy with Nusara hugging my waist from behind.

I looked back with surprise. What exactly did God have in mind for this trip? The beautiful Pan Borneo Highway was under construction. The motorcycle was held hostage. I got to spend quality time with many great new friends. The Ducati worked perfectly throughout the trip.

Perhaps God wanted to make my life more colorful, but I really don't know God's wishes. I just know that Nusara wanted something.

"Next time, go a little closer."

'A woman who has been pleased by a man since bygone days knows no bound
to her own satisfaction.'

Epilogue

Apart from the one-man tour company, I only met very friendly and helpful people -- the staff at every hotel, restaurant, the police officers, my friends who rode motorcycles together in our group, or even the tour company's van driver.

Whether I was riding in the morning, late afternoon, or evening, alone or in a group, I never felt any threat or hostility.

If you're thinking of visiting either West Malaysia or Borneo, which includes East Malaysia, Brunei and Indonesia, please don't let this one-man tour company distort your perception of good people, and good friendships. In fact, one good thing that the tour company did was strengthen the bond in our group -- the more problems we had, the stronger, our bond of friendship. Of all the tours I went on, this was the group with whom I formed the most lasting connection. We are still chatting in the WhatsApp group and still planning to meet and ride together. This is all thanks to the tour company.

However, of all the cities I've been, there is the most beautiful city I'd like to recommend. Let me boast a little that you must not miss this place, whether or not you ride a motorcycle. Frankly speaking, I have no vested interest in saying this. People are very friendly and helpful. The food is amazing. The roads are great, and there are plenty of tourist attractions. The climate is pleasant (in some periods) and there are so many coffee shops that even if you drink at one cafe per day, you won't visit them all in one year.

This city is called Chiang Mai.

Let me repeat again. I'm saying this without any vested interest in the matter.

Road Diary

Part 1 : LOGISTIC RIDE

	Starting Point	Drive Through	Destination	Distance (km.)
February 22, 2019	Hat Yai	Sadao checkpoint	Alor Setar	118.80
February 23, 2019	Alor Setar	Klang	Port Klang	536.40
			Total:	655.20

Part 2 : TOUR RIDE

	Starting Point	Drive Through	Destination	Distance (km.)
March 8, 2019	Kota Kinabalu	Warehouse	Kota Kinabalu	23.80
March 9, 2019	Kota Kinabalu	Tip of Borneo	Kota Kinabalu	401.60
March 10, 2019	Kota Kinabalu	Board the ferry	Labuan Island	187.60
March 11, 2019	Labuan Island	Brunei	Miri	245.10
March 12, 2019	Miri	Bintulu	Sibu	440.00
March 13, 2019	Sibu	Maludam	Kuching	318.70
March 14, 2019	Kuching	Biawak	Sambas	202.90
March 15, 2019	Sambas	Beach / Temple	Singkawang	119.30
March 16, 2019	Singkawang	Telok Melano	Kuching	384.70
			Total:	2,323.70

Part 3 : SELF RIDE

	Starting Point	Drive Through	Destination	Distance (km.)
March 17 2019	Kuching	Around Kuching	Kuching	284.50
March 18 2019	Kuching	Around Kuching	Port Kuching	24.00
			Total:	308.50

Part 4 : RUNAWAY RIDE

Runaway Ride	Starting Point	Drive Through	Destination	Distance (km.)
March 26, 2019	Port Klang	E1	Ipoh	257.00
March 27, 2019	Ipoh	R152	Hat Yai	383.00
			Total:	640.00

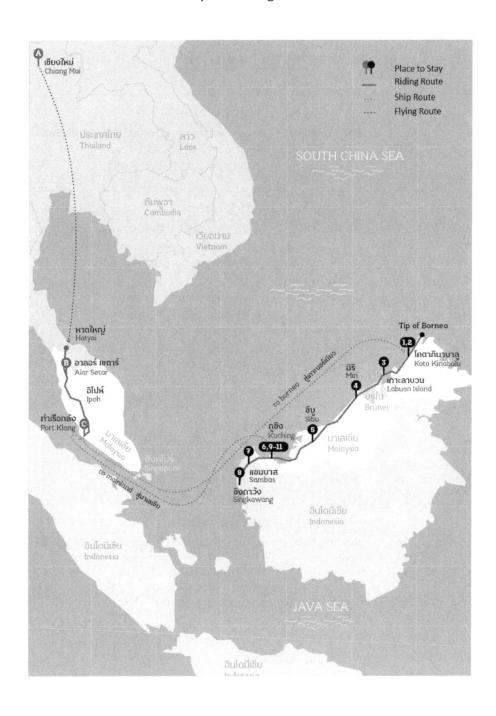

Shipping of the Motorcycle

From Port Klang (West Malaysia) to Kota Kinabalu (East Malaysia), I used ne service of Pos Logistics. For more information: www.poslogistics.com.my/solutions/vehicle-shipping-services.

On the way back, from Kuching (East Malaysia) back to Port Klang (West Malaysia), I used Giga Maritime Group. For more information:

- www.gmg.my

- www.facebook.com/GigaMaritimeGroup

Both ways, the transports were done on the RORO = Roll On / Roll Off basis, meaning riding the motorcycle on and off the ship with no need to pack it into a crate r container like normal shipping procedures. There's also no need to drain the petrol r remove the battery like air shipping. The motorcycle is in good condition, with no roblems or signs of damage whatsoever.

Endnote

[1] Mahathir Mohammad served as prime minister of Malaysia from 1981 to 2003. Subsequently, he reentered politics in 2018. His coalition of opposition parties or the Alliance of Hope (Pakatan Harapan – PH) won the election that year making him the world's oldest leader of a country at the age of 92 before resigning on February 24th 2020.

[2] Information from the 2018 Annual Report on the company website.

[3] The Malaysian political situations news came from The Borneo Post of March 8 2019. At that time, the Parti Pribumi Bersatu just won the election.

[4] On December 4, 2017, while taking a group photo with other cabinet members of the Prayuth 5 government, General Prawit Wongsuwan raised his hand to shield his face from the sun, and revealing a luxury watch valued at five million Baht on his wrist. This watch was not on his asset declaration submitted to The National Anti Corruption Commission (NACC). The incident was widely criticized on social media. More evidence had been dredged up. There were photos of General Prawit with over 20 luxury watches. When asked, he insisted that those watches were loaned to him by his friend named Patawat Suksriwong, aka Godfather Kram who had been his close friend for over 60 years and had been deceased. Later, the NACC ruled that there was not enough evidence to press charge against General Prawit for perjury, hence no subcommittee was formed to investigate the matter.

[5] "Returning Happiness to Thailand" is a song composed by General Prayuth Chanocha while heading the National Council for Peace and Order (NCPO). He finished the song in one hour and it was first aired in the Under the Thai Flag show on the Military radio station on June 6, 2514. The lyrics described General Prayuth's earnest intention to return happiness to the people.

[6] OCI - The Overseas Citizenship of India is a policy for citizens of India living outside of India to apply for this privilege by residing abroad, and having an Indian ancestor. The benefits are that no lifelong visa is required; they can go in and out of the country at any time without limitations; unlimited number of times for entries and exits of the country and no limit in duration of stays. They also are eligible to conduct business, occupy and hold almost equivalent assets to an Indian person. There are few exceptions for some occupations such as being farmers that are still reserved for Indians only. It is a policy that greatly promotes the Indian economy and tourism.

[7] Pan Borneo Highway or Trans Borneo Highway or Trans Kalimantan Highway is the main road on Borneo. It connects the two states of Malaysia which are Sabah and Sarawak, and stretches through Brunei and into Indonesia. Its total length is 5,324 kilometers, of which 2,083 kilometers are in Malaysia, 168 kilometers are in Brunei, and 3,073 kilometers in Indonesia. Its designation under the ASEAN highway network is AH150.

[8] Malaysia Truly Asia is a Malaysian tourism campaign that aimed to promote the "True Asia" spirit of Malaysia in the country's strength in the peaceful coexistence of the citizens with different ethnicities and religions.

[9] Amazing Thailand was a tourism promotion campaign by The Tourism Authority of Thailand (TAT) in foreign markets since 1999.

[10] Dato is a Malay title given to a person upon being conferred with certain orders of honor, for example, the Panglima Mahkota Wilayah (PMW), by the Malaysian government.

[11] The "Paris–Dakar" is an annual rally raid organized by the Amaury Sport Organisation. The course is so tough that riders/drivers and the vehicles are tested to their limits.

[12] The Commoners-Aristocrats discourse is a term that the Democratic Coalition against Dictatorship (UDD) or the Red Shirts used to show the polarized political struggle and reflect the lack of equality in Thai society. The commoners, represented as the Red Shirts are the ones who lack economic, political and social opportunities. The Aristocrat is the term coined by Thai academia to explain the ruling system in which the administrative power is in the hand of the civil servants, while the military power rests with the military.

[13] 911 refers to the Porsche 911 model, a two-door high-performance car. The boxer engine is positioned behind the rear wheels (rear engine) like the Volkswagen Beetle. Both of these cars were from the same designer, Dr. Ferdinand Porsche. Since its release in 1964 to the present, the Porsche 911 is still a high-performance two-door car. It's original design with rear Boxer engine, and round headlights has been maintained and captured the heart of many. It's hard to overlook if one wants to own a Porsche. (Author)

[14] Road 1148 National Highway No. 1148 (Tha Wang Pha - Chiang Kham) is the national highway between Tha Wang Pha District, Nan Province and Chiang Kham District, Phayao Province. This is one of the most scenic routes with the distance of about 113 kilometers. The winding of the road, the steep incline of the mountain, the surrounding lush greenery, and close to non-existent traffic is such a perfect combination that this road has received an unofficial high ranking from beautiful road guide websites in Thailand. It's often claimed that this road is great for those who live the open road life, be it in the cars or on the motorcycles and that they should try to drive along this road at least once. Nowadays, the other roads that are as famous are the 1256 and 1081, which have been unofficially nicknamed as 'Sky Highways', in Nan Province.

[15] "The protest is so much fun -- good food, great music" is the well-known sound bite of Kasit Piromya, Thailand's former Minister of Foreign Affairs who uttered this phrase on December 19, 2008, after the protest at Suvarnabhumi Airport disbanded. The protest was mobilized by The People's Alliance for Democracy (PAD) or the Yellow Shirts, a political group desiring to eradicate the Thaksin Shinawatra's

government and his networks. They moved to close Don Muang airport on November 24, 2008, and subsequently Suvarnabhumi Airport on November 25. The Kasikorn Research Center estimated that the occupation of both airports which had lasted ten days, cost the economy over two hundred billion baht of damage.

[16] *Carnet De Passages* are passports for automobiles or motorcycles to facilitate the transport of our vehicles or motorcycles across the countries. Safety deposits are required to be made at the Carnet's offices in each country. There is no need for further deposit or tax payment. The deposit is a guarantee of temporary import and that there will be no sales of the vehicles to evade taxation. (Source - www.carnetdepassage.org).

[17] We used the word 'Komodo dragon' to help readers visualize the event clearer, but, it was actually a 'Water monitor'. You may look up the different between these two on the internet.

About the Author

Rachant is a Thai of Indian descent who practices the Namdhari sect of Sikhism. Because he was born, raised and is still living in Chiang Mai, he prefers to call himself a 'Lanna native of Indian descent'.

During his childhood, Rachant used to sell fabrics, upholstery and linoleum at Warorot Market, which is known among the locals as "Gad Luang" (Central Market).

Growing up in the shophouses in Gad Luang, and meeting all kinds of people, he rarely had time to do anything else except minding the store. Yet, whenever his father's attention was elsewhere, he would disappear to get outside riding a motorcycle or driving a car -- living on the open road.

Workwise, he loves real estate development, construction, and the world of business.

His preferred lifestyle is living on the road on his motorcycles, and cars. Currently, he works mainly in real estate. He is a founding member of the Breakfast Biker Club, and most certainly still spending a lot of time on the road.

Rachant is still living in his beloved Chiang Mai, but no longer works at Gad Luang. He has become a nomad Lanna resident whose office is at a co-working space called Starwork, in the neighborhood with a strange name -- 'Thung Hotel' (a field full of hotels).

<u>Acknowledgement</u>

God - who works in mysterious ways beyond my ability to fathom.

My 'Srisakulchawla' family has enabled me to follow my very own path of happiness.

Nusara - who agreed to be the heroine of this book and of my life.

Sant Srisakulchawla, Rachin Srisakulchawla and Serene Srisakulchawla for smooth proof reading; to make sure the book is smooth for everyone to read

My Malaysian friends, who journeyed with me on this trip and who did not, but full of the love of life on two wheels, who gave me their friendship through thick and thin.

Printed in Great Britain
by Amazon

32285767R00139